745.53
H233c   cop.2

Hanauer.

Creating with leather.

A

Creating with LEATHER

Creating with LEATHER

By
Elsie Hanauer

South Brunswick and New York: A. S. Barnes and Company
London: Thomas Yoseloff Ltd

© 1970 by A. S. Barnes and Co., Inc.
Library of Congress Catalogue Card Number: 73-107115

A. S. Barnes and Co., Inc.
Cranbury, New Jersey 08512

Thomas Yoseloff Ltd
108 New Bond Street
London W1Y OQX, England

SBN 498 07620 2
Printed in the United States of America

Contents

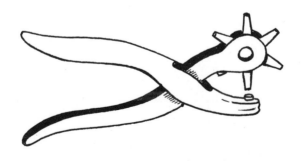

Creating
with
LEATHER

Leather

MOST ALL OF THE LEATHER TO BE USED FOR THE VARIOUS PROJECTS DESCRIBED ON THE FOLLOWING PAGES IS THE NATURAL-COLORED TOOLING TYPE. THIS LEATHER, TANNED BY A SPECIAL PROCESS, OFFERS A FIRM BODY, FINE GRAINED SURFACE AND DURABILITY.

YOU WILL NOTE THAT EACH PROJECT SPECIFIES THE WEIGHT OF LEATHER THAT SHOULD BE USED. THE THICKNESS OF MOST ALL LEATHER IS MEASURED IN OUNCES, AS ILLUSTRATED ON THE CHART BELOW.

3-4 OUNCE	7-8 OUNCE
4-5 OUNCE	8-9 OUNCE
5-6 OUNCE	9-10 OUNCE
6-7 OUNCE	10-11 OUNCE

THE LEATHER OFFERED BY MAIL-ORDER SALE IS DESCRIBED HONESTLY AS TO SIZE, COLOR AND GRADE. IT MUST BE REMEMBERED THAT LEATHER IS NOT MANUFACTURED LIKE CLOTH, SO IT OFTEN VARIES IN COLOR AND THICKNESS. SCARS AND SCRATCHES MAY ALSO BE PRESENT, ESPECIALLY ON HIDES GRADED "C" OR "D". THE HIDES WHICH ARE "B" GRADE ARE THE MOST POPULAR CHOICE.

Tools

ALL YOU WILL NEED TO MAKE THE VARIETY OF LEATHER ITEMS FOUND IN THIS BOOK IS A ROTARY TYPE LEATHER PUNCH, AN X-ACTO TYPE KNIFE AND A WHITE GLUE.

THE ROTARY TYPE LEATHER PUNCH OFFERS SIX DIFFERENT DRIVE TUBE SIZES. IT'S REALLY SIX LEATHER PUNCHES, ALL IN ONE.

THE X-ACTO TYPE KNIFE OFFERS A SURGICAL SHARP BLADE, WHICH IS MOST IMPORTANT FOR A CLEAN CUT. THE X-ACTO ALSO OFFERS A VARIETY OF DIFFERENT SHAPED BLADES, BUT IN MOST CASES, THE BLADE SHOWN IS THE ONLY ONE REQUIRED.

WHITE GLUE WILL BOND LEATHER TO MOST ANY TYPE OF SURFACE. IT HAS NO OFFENSIVE ODOR, DRIES QUICKLY AND A LITTLE GOES A LONG WAY.

Patterns

TO OBTAIN THE PATTERNS FROM THIS BOOK WITH-
OUT MARRING OR DESTROYING THE PAGES, IT IS
SUGGESTED THAT A TRANSPARENT TRACING
PAPER AND A SOFT PENCIL BE USED.

ONCE ALL PIECES OF THE PATTERN HAVE BEEN
TRACED ONTO THE TRACING PAPER, TRANSFER
THEM TO A HEAVY PIECE OF PAPER BY RETRACING
OVER A CARBON PAPER WITH A HARD PENCIL.
CUT OUT THE PATTERNS WITH A SHARP KNIFE
AND THEN NUMBER EACH PIECE.

WHEN A PATTERN HAS SEVERAL DIFFERENT PIECES
IT MAY BE A GOOD IDEA TO FASTEN THEM ALL
TOGETHER WITH A LARGE PAPER CLIP OR DROP
THEM INTO AN ENVELOPE TO PREVENT LOSS.

SPREAD THE LEATHER TO BE USED OUT FLAT ON A
BOARD OR PIECE OF MASONITE. LAY PATTERNS
ON THE LEATHER, BUT BE SURE TO AVOID LAYING
THE PIECES ON ANY FLAWS OR SCRATCHES IN
THE LEATHER. TRACE AROUND THE PATTERNS WITH
A HARD PENCIL, BEING CAREFUL THAT PATTERNS
DO NOT MOVE. CAREFULLY CUT OUT ALL PIECES
WITH THE X-ACTO KNIFE.

IF, WHILE CUTTING OUT THE PATTERNS, YOUR KNIFE
SHOULD SLIP AND CUT INTO THE LEATHER WHERE
IT SHOULDN'T, DISCARD THE PIECE AND CUT OUT A
NEW ONE. REMEMBER, ONE PATTERN PIECE CUT
WRONG CAN RUIN THE WHOLE PROJECT.

Coloring

THE LIQUID POSTER PAINTS MAY BE USED FOR COLOR-
ING MANY OF THE FINISHED PROJECTS IN THIS BOOK.
THESE PAINTS ARE AVAILABLE IN SETS OF 12 ONE-
OUNCE BOTTLES AT A MODERATE PRICE.

ALL THE LEATHER PROJECTS THAT WILL RECEIVE
CONSIDERABLE HANDLING OR WEAR SHOULD BE
COLORED WITH A GOOD LEATHER DYE. LIKE THE
POSTER PAINTS, LEATHER DYE IS ALSO AVAILABLE
IN SETS OF ASSORTED COLORS, BUT AT A SLIGHTLY
HIGHER PRICE.

THE PROJECTS PAINTED WITH THE POSTER COLORS
SHOULD BE SPRAYED WITH ONE OR MORE COATS
OF CLEAR LACQUER. THIS WILL PROTECT FROM SOIL
AND ALSO PREVENT THE COLORS FROM SMUDGE.
REMEMBER THAT SEVERAL LIGHT COATS OF THE
LACQUER WILL OFFER A BETTER FINISH THAN ONE
HEAVY COAT.

FOR COLORING WITH DYE OR POSTER PAINT, USE
ONLY GOOD SABLE BRUSHES. FOR FINE DETAIL
YOU WILL NEED A NUMBER 2 BRUSH. FOR LARGE
AREAS USE A ¼" BRUSH.

FOR COLORING LARGE AREAS.

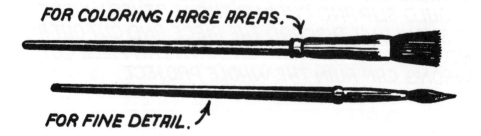

FOR FINE DETAIL.

Pencil Holder

TO MAKE THE PENCIL HOLDER SHOWN BELOW, YOU
WILL NEED AN EMPTY TIN CAN THAT MEASURES
4 INCHES HIGH AND 2½ INCHES ACROSS THE
TOP. CAMPBELL'S SOUP CANS ARE THE RIGHT SIZE
AND EASY TO FIND.

FOLLOW THE STEP-
BY-STEP DIRECTIONS
GIVEN ON THE NEXT
TWO PAGES.

THE #1 PIECE MAY
BE LEFT NATURAL
AND THE DESIGN
PAINTED ON WITH
EITHER BLACK OR
A DARK BROWN.
ALSO COLOR THE
BASE PIECES TO
MATCH AS SHOWN.

WHEN THE PENCIL
HOLDER HAS BEEN
FULLY ASSEMBLED,
SPRAY IT LIGHTLY
WITH CLEAR LACQUER.

#1
#2
#4
#3

1.

#2 CUT
BOTH PIECES
1 AND 2
SLIGHTLY
LONGER
THAN
SHOWN.
FIT TO
CAN AND
TRIM OFF
EXCESS.

CUT BOTH
PATTERNS
FROM 3
OUNCE
LEATHER.

THE DESIGN
SHOULD BE
COMPLETED
BEFORE #1
IS GLUED
ON CAN.

THE DESIGN
MAY BE
CUT FROM
ANOTHER
PIECE OF
LEATHER
AND GLUED
ON, OR IT
MAY BE
PAINTED
ON.

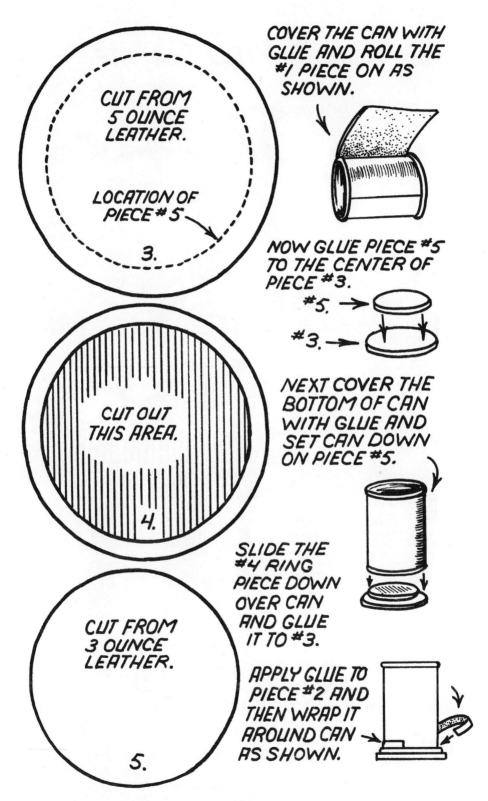

CUT FROM
5 OUNCE
LEATHER.

LOCATION OF
PIECE #5

3.

CUT OUT
THIS AREA.

4.

CUT FROM
3 OUNCE
LEATHER.

5.

COVER THE CAN WITH GLUE AND ROLL THE #1 PIECE ON AS SHOWN.

NOW GLUE PIECE #5 TO THE CENTER OF PIECE #3.

#5.

#3.

NEXT COVER THE BOTTOM OF CAN WITH GLUE AND SET CAN DOWN ON PIECE #5.

SLIDE THE #4 RING PIECE DOWN OVER CAN AND GLUE IT TO #3.

APPLY GLUE TO PIECE #2 AND THEN WRAP IT AROUND CAN AS SHOWN.

Patio Wind Chime

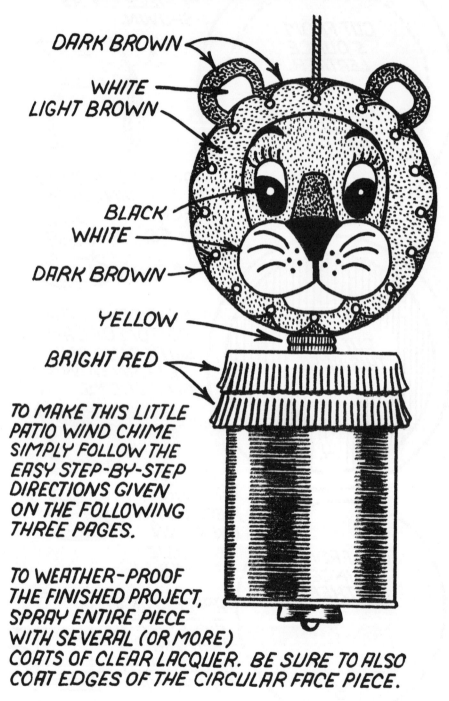

DARK BROWN

WHITE
LIGHT BROWN

BLACK
WHITE

DARK BROWN

YELLOW

BRIGHT RED

TO MAKE THIS LITTLE PATIO WIND CHIME SIMPLY FOLLOW THE EASY STEP-BY-STEP DIRECTIONS GIVEN ON THE FOLLOWING THREE PAGES.

TO WEATHER-PROOF THE FINISHED PROJECT, SPRAY ENTIRE PIECE WITH SEVERAL (OR MORE) COATS OF CLEAR LACQUER. BE SURE TO ALSO COAT EDGES OF THE CIRCULAR FACE PIECE.

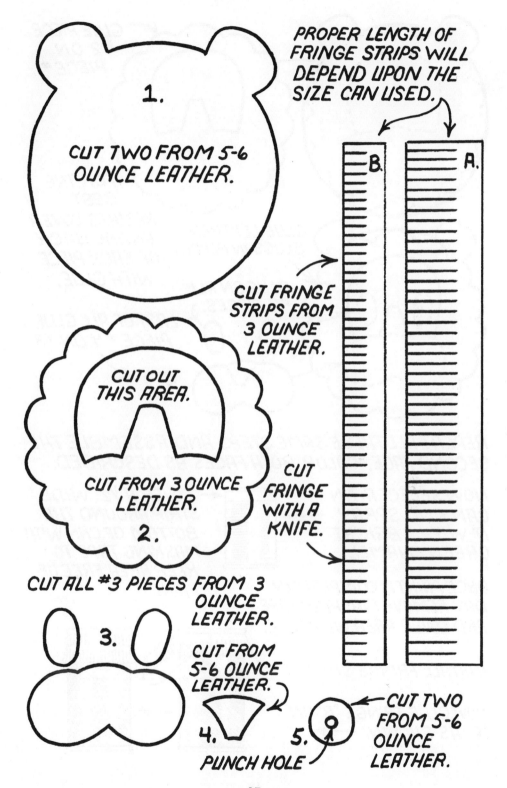

1.

CUT TWO FROM 5-6 OUNCE LEATHER.

PROPER LENGTH OF FRINGE STRIPS WILL DEPEND UPON THE SIZE CAN USED.

B.

A.

CUT FRINGE STRIPS FROM 3 OUNCE LEATHER.

CUT OUT THIS AREA.

CUT FROM 3 OUNCE LEATHER.

2.

CUT FRINGE WITH A KNIFE.

CUT ALL #3 PIECES FROM 3 OUNCE LEATHER.

3.

CUT FROM 5-6 OUNCE LEATHER.

4.

PUNCH HOLE

5.

CUT TWO FROM 5-6 OUNCE LEATHER.

17

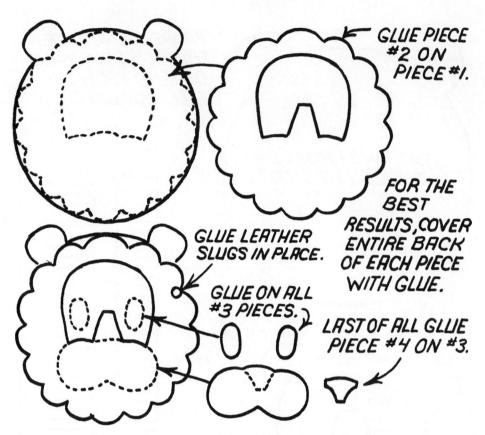

GLUE PIECE #2 ON PIECE #1.

FOR THE BEST RESULTS, COVER ENTIRE BACK OF EACH PIECE WITH GLUE.

GLUE LEATHER SLUGS IN PLACE.

GLUE ON ALL #3 PIECES.

LAST OF ALL GLUE PIECE #4 ON #3.

REPEAT ALL THESE SAME STEPS AND ASSEMBLE THE SECOND FACE. COLOR BOTH FACES AS DESCRIBED.

NOW SELECT A TIN CAN AND SPRAY IT WITH A BRIGHT GREEN ENAMEL.

COVER A ½" WIDE STRIP AROUND THE BOTTOM OF CAN WITH MASKING TAPE TO KEEP AREA FREE OF PAINT.

ONCE PAINT IS COMPLETELY DRY, REMOVE MASKING TAPE AND COVER AREA WITH GLUE.

INSTALL FRINGE STRIP "A".

NOW GLUE FRINGE "B" ON "A" AS SHOWN. →

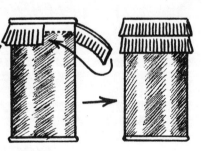

NOW YOU WILL NEED A PIECE OF HEAVY CORD BETWEEN 12 AND 15 INCHES LONG. TIE A SMALL METAL BELL TIGHTLY TO ONE END OF THIS CORD.

NEXT MEASURE LENGTH OF THE CAN AND TIE A LARGE DOUBLE KNOT IN CORD SO THAT THE BELL WILL HANG 1/2" BELOW THE CAN AS SHOWN. →

SLIDE THE TWO #5 PIECES ON THE CORD AS SHOWN.

COVER THE BACK OF BOTH FACE PIECES WITH GLUE, LAY CORD ACROSS ONE AND THEN CAREFULLY PLACE THE TWO HALVES TOGETHER.

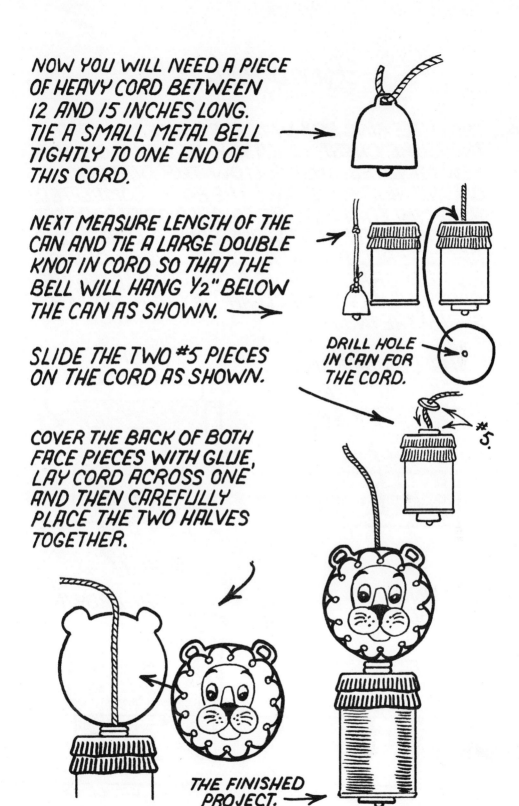

DRILL HOLE IN CAN FOR THE CORD.

#5.

THE FINISHED PROJECT. →

Ring Box

THE LITTLE RING BOX, WHICH IS SHAPED LIKE A TREASURE CHEST, IS EASILY MADE IN ONLY A FEW MINUTES. JUST FOLLOW THE DIRECTIONS ON THE NEXT PAGE. ONCE THE BOX IS COMPLETELY ASSEMBLED IT MAY BE COLORED OR DECORATED IN MANY DIFFERENT WAYS. SOME SUGGESTIONS ARE OFFERED BELOW. AFTER ALL THE COLORING AND DECORATING HAVE BEEN COMPLETED, THEN SPRAY LIGHTLY WITH CLEAR LACQUER. DO NOT SPRAY THE INSIDE.

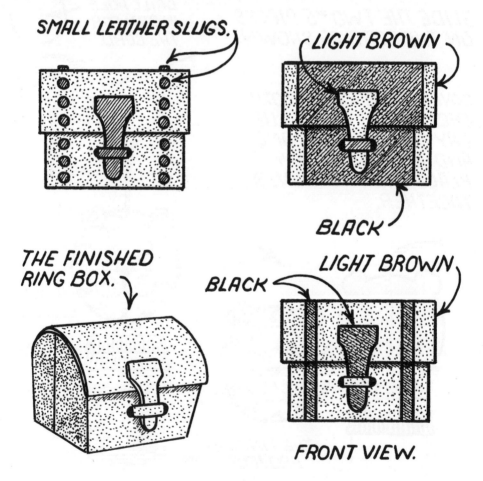

SMALL LEATHER SLUGS.

LIGHT BROWN

BLACK

THE FINISHED RING BOX.

BLACK

LIGHT BROWN

FRONT VIEW.

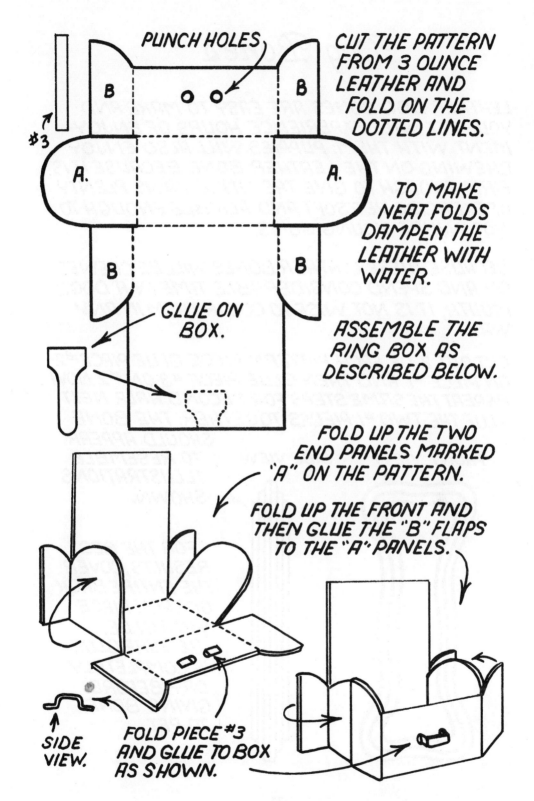

PUNCH HOLES

CUT THE PATTERN FROM 3 OUNCE LEATHER AND FOLD ON THE DOTTED LINES.

B   B

#3

A.   A.

TO MAKE NEAT FOLDS DAMPEN THE LEATHER WITH WATER.

B   B

GLUE ON BOX.

ASSEMBLE THE RING BOX AS DESCRIBED BELOW.

FOLD UP THE TWO END PANELS MARKED "A" ON THE PATTERN.

FOLD UP THE FRONT AND THEN GLUE THE "B" FLAPS TO THE "A" PANELS.

SIDE VIEW.

FOLD PIECE #3 AND GLUE TO BOX AS SHOWN.

Dog Bones

LEATHER DOG BONES ARE EASY TO MAKE AND YOUR PET WILL EXPERIENCE HOURS OF ENJOYMENT WITH THEM. PUPPIES WILL ALSO ENJOY CHEWING ON THE LEATHER BONE BECAUSE IT IS FIRM ENOUGH TO GIVE THE LITTLE JAWS PLENTY OF EXERCISE YET SOFT AND PLIABLE ENOUGH TO NOT INJURE YOUNG GUMS.

BECAUSE THESE LEATHER BONES WILL BE CHEWED ON AND SPEND CONSIDERABLE TIME IN A DOG'S MOUTH, IT IS NOT WISE TO COLOR THEM IN ANY WAY.

CUT OUT 2 OF EACH PATTERN PIECE. GLUE PIECE #2 ON PIECE #1 AND THEN GLUE PIECE #3 ON #2. NOW REPEAT THE SAME STEPS FOR SECOND HALF. NEXT GLUE THE TWO #1 PIECES TOGETHER. THE BONE SHOULD APPEAR TO RESEMBLE ILLUSTRATIONS SHOWN.

FRONT VIEW   SIDE VIEW

FOR THE BEST RESULTS, COVER THE ENTIRE BACK OF EACH PIECE WITH GLUE. BE SURE GLUE IS COMPLETELY DRY BEFORE GIVING BONE TO PET.

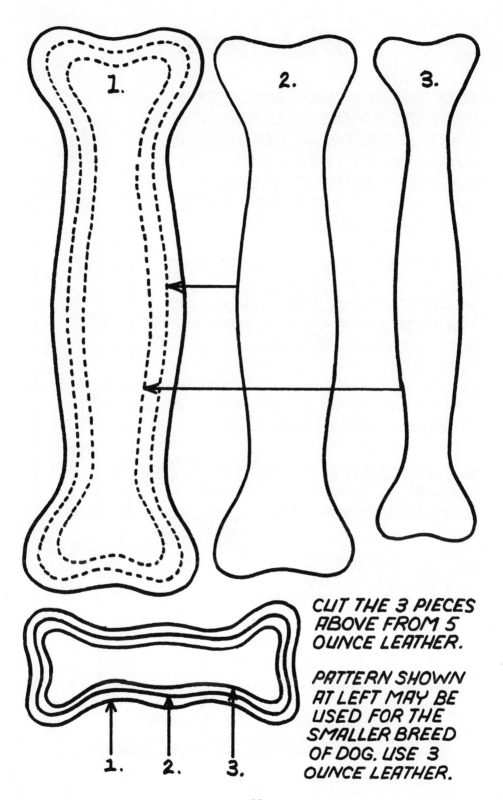

CUT THE 3 PIECES
ABOVE FROM 5
OUNCE LEATHER.

PATTERN SHOWN
AT LEFT MAY BE
USED FOR THE
SMALLER BREED
OF DOG. USE 3
OUNCE LEATHER.

Watchbands

NOTE THAT THE TWO WATCHBAND
PATTERNS ON THE NEXT PAGE ARE
FOR TWO DIFFERENT SIZE WATCHES.
THE NUMBER 1 PATTERN IS FOR
THE SMALL SPORT TYPE WATCH.
THE NUMBER 2 PATTERN IS FOR
THE LARGE MAN'S WATCH.

CUT OUT BOTH THE "A" AND "B" PIECES
AND THEN CUT THE 8 STRAP SLOTS
IN PIECE "A." PIECE "A" MAY BE LEFT
PLAIN OR DESIGNS CUT OUT AS
SUGGESTED ON PATTERNS. THE
TWO PIECES MAY BE DYED IN ANY
COLOR OF YOUR CHOICE OR LEFT
NATURAL. WAX OR SPRAY SURFACE
OF BOTH PIECES WITH LACQUER.

NOW INSTALL THE
BUCKLE ON STRAP
"B" AS SHOWN. →

SMALL
RIVET.

INSERT THE WATCH
IN BAND AS SHOWN
IN THE SIDE VIEW SKETCH.

BUCKLE   WATCH   "STRAP "B"

←"STRAP "A"

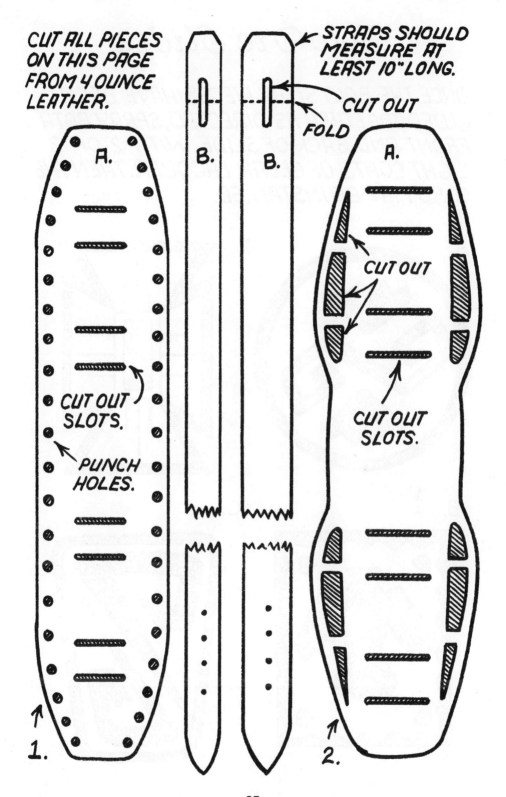

CUT ALL PIECES ON THIS PAGE FROM 4 OUNCE LEATHER.

STRAPS SHOULD MEASURE AT LEAST 10" LONG.

A.

B.

B.

CUT OUT

FOLD

A.

CUT OUT

CUT OUT SLOTS.

PUNCH HOLES.

CUT OUT SLOTS.

1.

2.

25

Bolo Tie Slides

ONCE THE BOLO SLIDE PIECES HAVE BEEN GLUED TOGETHER AS DIRECTED, SPRAY BOTH FRONT AND BACK OF SLIDE WITH 2 OR 3 LIGHT COATS OF CLEAR LACQUER. THEN THE CORD MAY BE INSTALLED.

A.

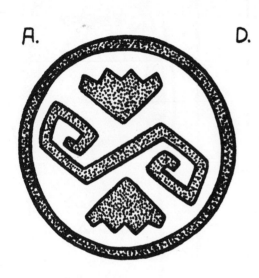

D.

B.

C.

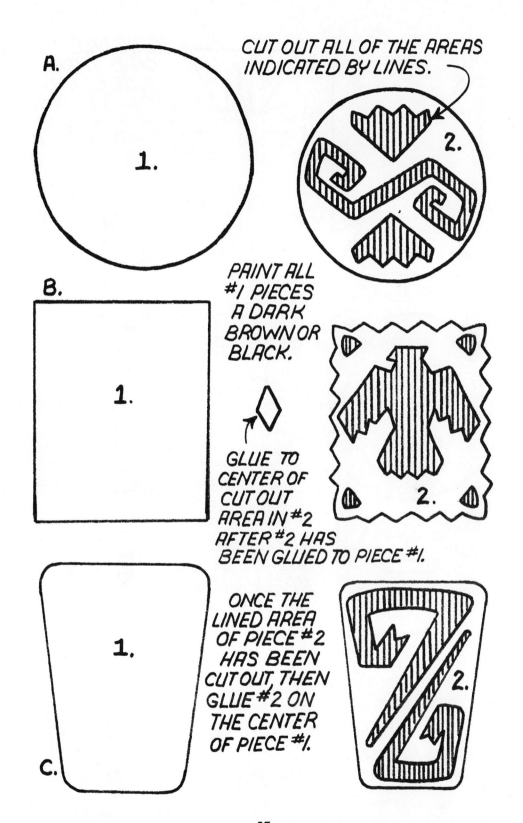

A.

1.

CUT OUT ALL OF THE AREAS INDICATED BY LINES.

2.

PAINT ALL #1 PIECES A DARK BROWN OR BLACK.

B.

1.

GLUE TO CENTER OF CUT OUT AREA IN #2 AFTER #2 HAS BEEN GLUED TO PIECE #1.

2.

ONCE THE LINED AREA OF PIECE #2 HAS BEEN CUT OUT, THEN GLUE #2 ON THE CENTER OF PIECE #1.

1.

C.

2.

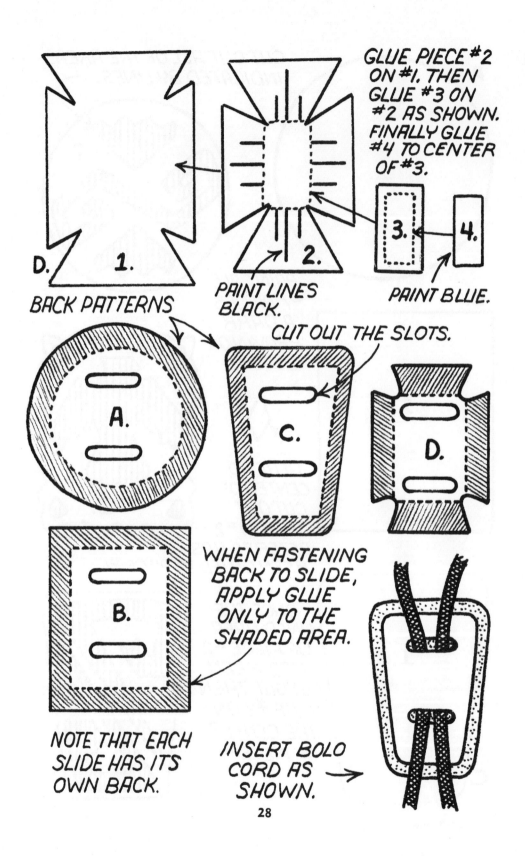

GLUE PIECE #2 ON #1. THEN GLUE #3 ON #2 AS SHOWN. FINALLY GLUE #4 TO CENTER OF #3.

D. 1.

BACK PATTERNS

2.

PAINT LINES BLACK.

3. 4.

PAINT BLUE.

CUT OUT THE SLOTS.

A. C. D.

B.

WHEN FASTENING BACK TO SLIDE, APPLY GLUE ONLY TO THE SHADED AREA.

NOTE THAT EACH SLIDE HAS ITS OWN BACK.

INSERT BOLO CORD AS SHOWN.

Cigarette Case

TO MAKE THE CIGARETTE CASE SHOWN BELOW
YOU WILL NEED ONE STANDARD SIZE BAND-AID
BOX. COVER THE OUTSIDE OF ENTIRE TOP AND
AREA ON FRONT OF CAN WITH A VARNISH AND
PAINT REMOVER. WHEN ALL THE PAINT IN THE
INDICATED AREAS HAS BEEN REMOVED, RUB
WITH A FINE GRADE OF STEEL WOOL. THIS WILL
GIVE THE METAL A BRUSHED CHROME LOOK.
NOW GLUE THE LEATHER PIECE TO THE CAN.

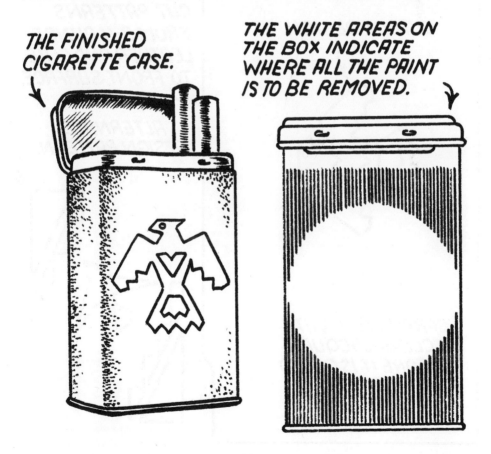

THE FINISHED
CIGARETTE CASE.

THE WHITE AREAS ON
THE BOX INDICATE
WHERE ALL THE PAINT
IS TO BE REMOVED.

FRONT OF COVERED CAN.

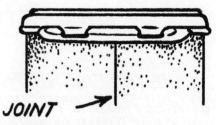

JOINT

BACK OF COVERED CAN.

← CUT PATTERN FROM 3 OUNCE LEATHER.

CUTOUT DESIGN.

IF A RAISED TYPE DESIGN IS DESIRED, CUT PATTERNS FROM 3-4 OUNCE LEATHER AND GLUE TO FRONT SURFACE.

ALTERNATE DESIGN PATTERN.

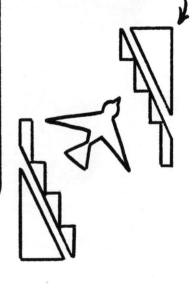

SPRAY PIECE WITH A CLEAR LACQUER BEFORE IT IS GLUED ON THE BOX.

Match Book Case

TO MAKE THE ATTRACTIVE MATCH BOOK CASE
ILLUSTRATED BELOW, FOLLOW THE STEP-BY-STEP
INSTRUCTIONS ON THE FOLLOWING PAGES.

THE MATCH BOOK CASE MAY BE LEFT PLAIN OR A
DESIGN MAY BE USED. IN THE EVENT THAT A
DESIGN IS TO BE USED, IT SHOULD BE APPLIED
BEFORE THE CASE IS ASSEMBLED. DAMPEN THE
#1 PIECE WITH WATER AND TRACE THE DESIGN
ON THE LEATHER WITH A HARD PENCIL. THIS WILL
GIVE A PERMANENT OUTLINE
OF THE DESIGN IN THE
LEATHER. THE DESIGN
MAY BE COLORED OR
LEFT NATURAL. SPRAY
SURFACE WITH 2 OR 3
LIGHT COATS OF CLEAR
LACQUER.

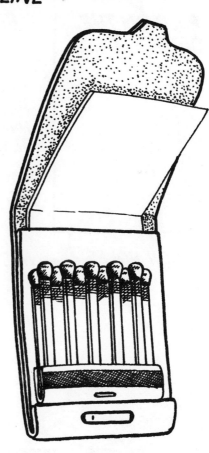

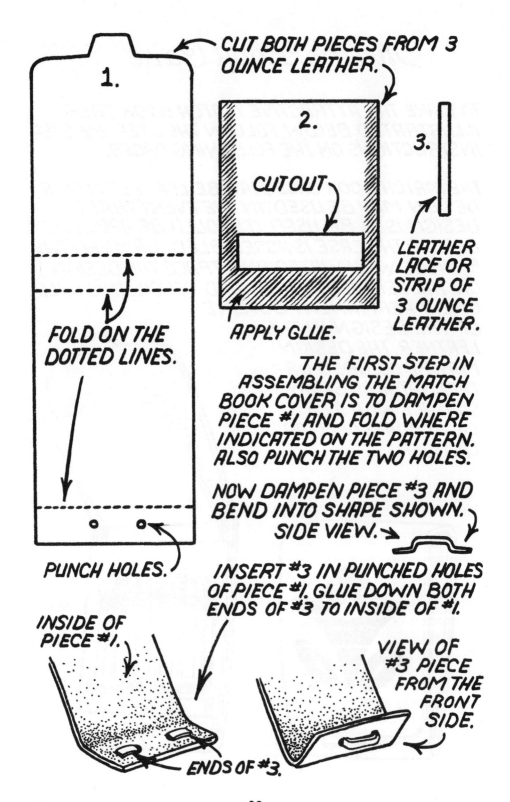

CUT BOTH PIECES FROM 3 OUNCE LEATHER.

1.

2.

3.

CUT OUT

LEATHER LACE OR STRIP OF 3 OUNCE LEATHER.

FOLD ON THE DOTTED LINES.

APPLY GLUE.

THE FIRST STEP IN ASSEMBLING THE MATCH BOOK COVER IS TO DAMPEN PIECE #1 AND FOLD WHERE INDICATED ON THE PATTERN. ALSO PUNCH THE TWO HOLES.

PUNCH HOLES.

NOW DAMPEN PIECE #3 AND BEND INTO SHAPE SHOWN. SIDE VIEW. →

INSERT #3 IN PUNCHED HOLES OF PIECE #1. GLUE DOWN BOTH ENDS OF #3 TO INSIDE OF #1.

INSIDE OF PIECE #1.

VIEW OF #3 PIECE FROM THE FRONT SIDE.

ENDS OF #3.

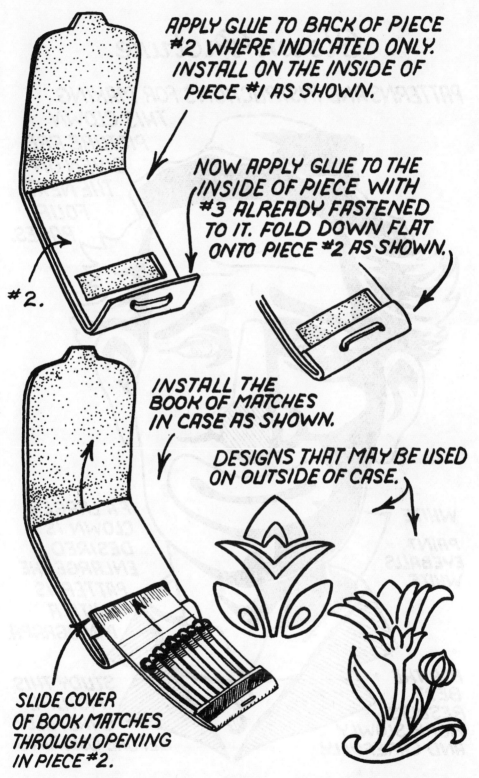

APPLY GLUE TO BACK OF PIECE #2 WHERE INDICATED ONLY. INSTALL ON THE INSIDE OF PIECE #1 AS SHOWN.

NOW APPLY GLUE TO THE INSIDE OF PIECE WITH #3 ALREADY FASTENED TO IT. FOLD DOWN FLAT ONTO PIECE #2 AS SHOWN.

#2.

INSTALL THE BOOK OF MATCHES IN CASE AS SHOWN.

DESIGNS THAT MAY BE USED ON OUTSIDE OF CASE.

SLIDE COVER OF BOOK MATCHES THROUGH OPENING IN PIECE #2.

33

Clown Picture

PATTERNS AND INSTRUCTIONS FOR MAKING THIS CLOWN PICTURE ARE GIVEN ON THE NEXT FOUR PAGES.

WHITE

PAINT EYEBALLS WHITE.

IF A LARGER CLOWN IS DESIRED ENLARGE THE PATTERNS WITH A PANTOGRAPH.

FOR THE BEST RESULTS, WORK SLOWLY AND CAREFULLY.

STUDY THIS PICTURE CAREFULLY BEFORE COLORING.

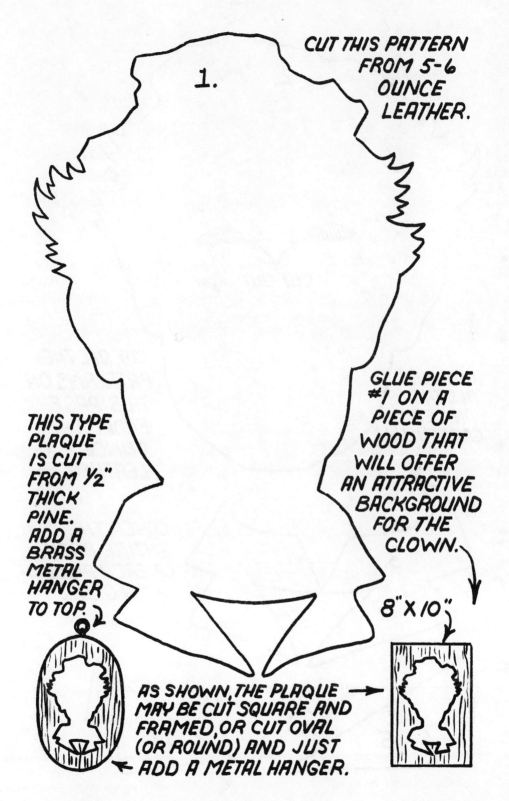

CUT THIS PATTERN FROM 5-6 OUNCE LEATHER.

1.

GLUE PIECE #1 ON A PIECE OF WOOD THAT WILL OFFER AN ATTRACTIVE BACKGROUND FOR THE CLOWN.

THIS TYPE PLAQUE IS CUT FROM 1/2" THICK PINE. ADD A BRASS METAL HANGER TO TOP.

8" X 10"

AS SHOWN, THE PLAQUE MAY BE CUT SQUARE AND FRAMED, OR CUT OVAL (OR ROUND) AND JUST ADD A METAL HANGER.

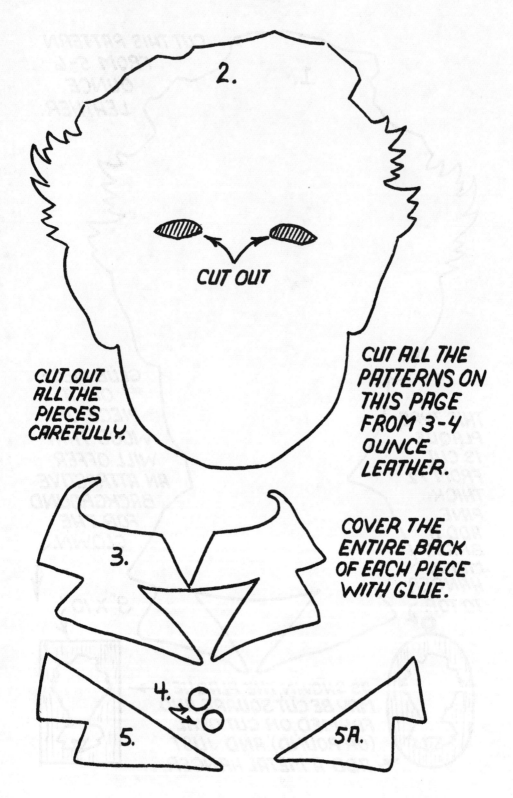

2.

CUT OUT

CUT OUT
ALL THE
PIECES
CAREFULLY.

CUT ALL THE
PATTERNS ON
THIS PAGE
FROM 3-4
OUNCE
LEATHER.

3.

COVER THE
ENTIRE BACK
OF EACH PIECE
WITH GLUE.

4.

5.

5A.

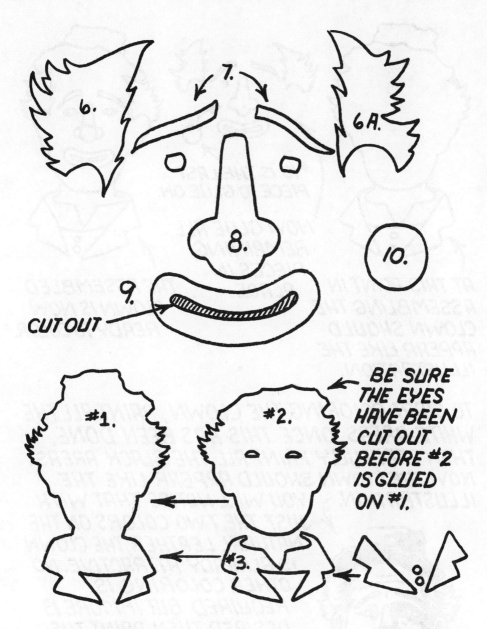

7.

6. 6A.

8.

10.

9.

CUT OUT

#1. #2. BE SURE
THE EYES
HAVE BEEN
CUT OUT
BEFORE #2
IS GLUED
ON #1.

#3.

ONCE PIECE #1 HAS BEEN GLUED ON THE WOOD
(OR MASONITE) BACKGROUND, THE OTHER
PIECES MAY BE GLUED IN POSITION. START WITH
PIECE #2 AND GLUE IT ON #1 AS SHOWN. NOW
GLUE #3 ON #1. THEN GLUE PIECES #5 AND #5A
IN PLACE. ALSO GLUE PIECES #4 IN PLACE.

#10 IS THE LAST PIECE TO GLUE ON.

NOW GLUE ALL REMAINING PIECES IN PLACE.

AT THIS POINT IN ASSEMBLING THE CLOWN SHOULD APPEAR LIKE THE ILLUSTRATION.

THE ASSEMBLED CLOWN IS NOW READY TO COLOR.

TO START COLORING THE CLOWN, PAINT ALL THE WHITE AREAS. ONCE THIS HAS BEEN DONE, THEN CAREFULLY PAINT ALL THE BLACK AREAS. NOW THE CLOWN SHOULD APPEAR LIKE THE ILLUSTRATION.

YOU WILL NOTICE THAT WITH JUST THE TWO COLORS ON THE NATURAL LEATHER, THE CLOWN IS ALREADY ATTRACTIVE. NO OTHER COLORING IS REQUIRED BUT IF MORE IS DESIRED THEN PAINT THE FACE A FLESH TONE AND THE NOSE A BRIGHT RED. THE EYES ARE BLUE. THE HAT IS GREEN AND THE JACKET IS BROWN. COLOR THE HAIR A REDDISH SHADE OF BROWN.

Bracelets

PATTERNS FOR THE LEATHER BRACELETS SHOWN
BELOW ARE GIVEN ON THE FOLLOWING PAGES.
FOLLOW ASSEMBLY INSTRUCTIONS CAREFULLY
AND THEN COLOR. SUGGESTED COLORS ARE
GIVEN, BUT THE BRACELETS MAY BE COLORED
IN MANY DIFFERENT SHADES TO SUIT THE
INDIVIDUAL. THE EDGES OF THE ORNAMENTS,
AS WELL AS THE FLAT SURFACE, SHOULD BE
COLORED FOR A MORE EFFECTIVE APPEARANCE.
TO AVOID GETTING COLOR ON THE BRACELET,
COLOR THE ORNAMENTS BEFORE THEY ARE
GLUED IN PLACE.

CUT THE BRACELET
PATTERNS FROM
2-3 OUNCE LEATHER.

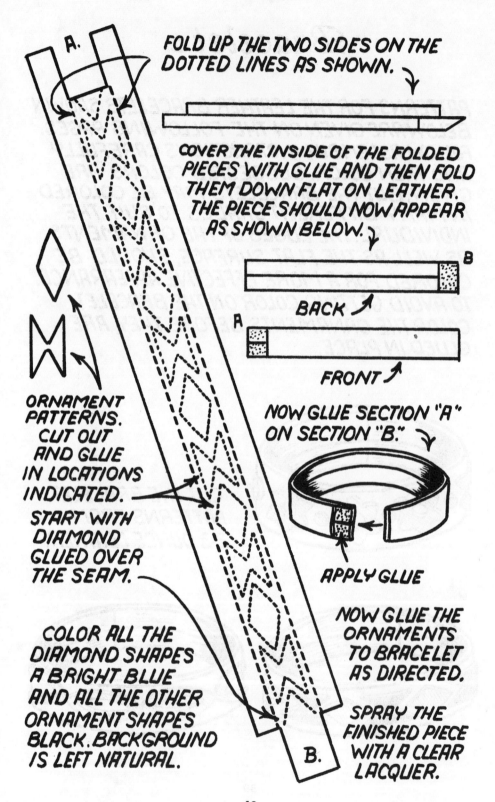

A.

FOLD UP THE TWO SIDES ON THE DOTTED LINES AS SHOWN.

COVER THE INSIDE OF THE FOLDED PIECES WITH GLUE AND THEN FOLD THEM DOWN FLAT ON LEATHER. THE PIECE SHOULD NOW APPEAR AS SHOWN BELOW.

B

BACK

A

FRONT

ORNAMENT PATTERNS. CUT OUT AND GLUE IN LOCATIONS INDICATED.

START WITH DIAMOND GLUED OVER THE SEAM.

NOW GLUE SECTION "A" ON SECTION "B."

APPLY GLUE

NOW GLUE THE ORNAMENTS TO BRACELET AS DIRECTED.

COLOR ALL THE DIAMOND SHAPES A BRIGHT BLUE AND ALL THE OTHER ORNAMENT SHAPES BLACK. BACKGROUND IS LEFT NATURAL.

SPRAY THE FINISHED PIECE WITH A CLEAR LACQUER.

B.

THE BRACELET PATTERNS SHOWN BELOW ARE ASSEMBLED IN THE SAME WAY AS THE ONE DESCRIBED ON THE PRECEDING PAGE. MATCH DOTTED LINES "A" AND "B" TO MAKE PATTERNS ONE PIECE.

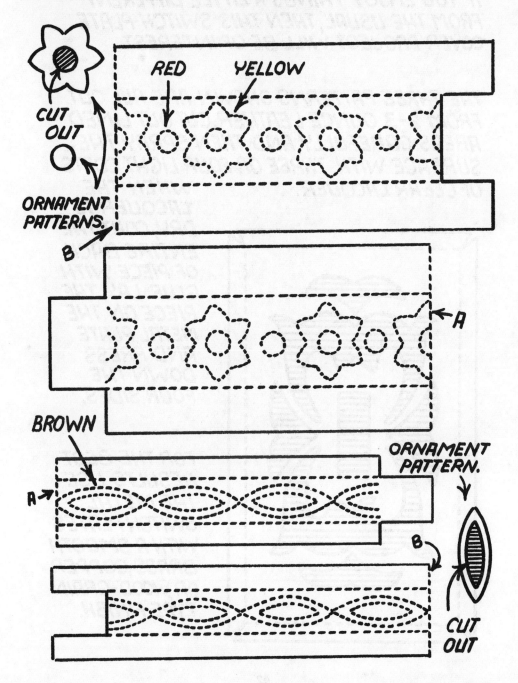

CUT OUT

RED   YELLOW

ORNAMENT PATTERNS.

B

A

BROWN

ORNAMENT PATTERN.

A

B

CUT OUT

41

Switch Plate Covers

IF YOU ENJOY THINGS A LITTLE DIFFERENT FROM THE USUAL, THEN THIS SWITCH PLATE COVER PROJECT WILL BE OF INTEREST.

THE THREE PATTERNS SHOWN ARE ALL CUT FROM 2-3 OUNCE LEATHER. CUT OUT LINED AREAS CAREFULLY AND THEN SPRAY THE SURFACE WITH THREE OR FOUR LIGHT COATS OF CLEAR LACQUER.

WHEN THE LACQUER IS DRY, COAT THE ENTIRE BACK OF PIECE WITH GLUE. LAY THE PIECE ON THE METAL PLATE AND PRESS DOWN THE FOUR SIDES.

FOR THE BEST RESULTS USE THE METAL SWITCH PLATES WITH A SMOOTH BRASS, COPPER OR WOOD-GRAIN TYPE FINISH.

THE DOTTED LINES ON THE
PATTERNS INDICATE WHERE
LEATHER IS TO BE PRESSED
DOWN OVER SIDES OF PLATE.

LEATHER COVERS
MAY BE COLORED
IF DESIRED.

END VIEW OF A
METAL SWITCH PLATE.

SIDE

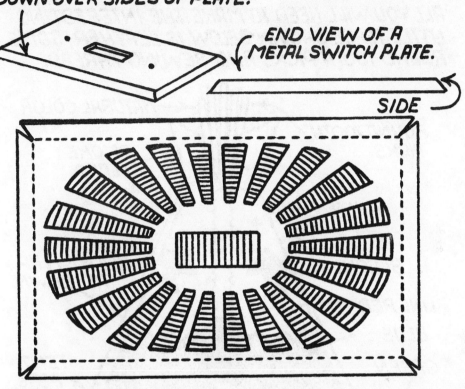

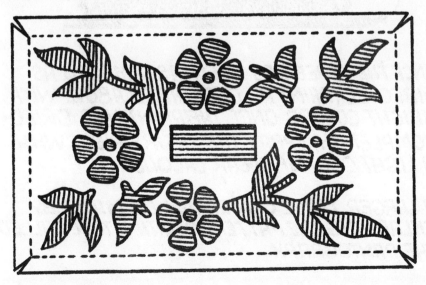

43

Miniature Tepee

ALL YOU WILL NEED TO MAKE THE INTERESTING LITTLE TEPEE SHOWN BELOW IS LEATHER, SOME ROUND TOOTH PICKS AND SEWING THREAD.

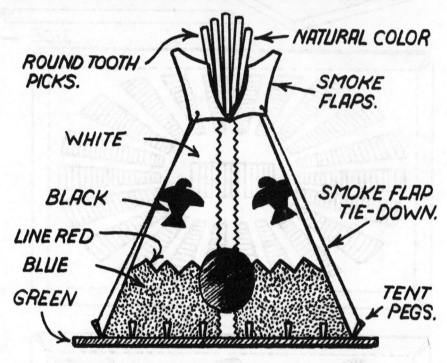

ONCE THE TEPEE HAS BEEN ASSEMBLED AS DIRECTED, PAINT AS DESCRIBED ABOVE WITH BRIGHT COLORS. ONCE THE PAINT HAS DRIED COMPLETELY, SPRAY THE ENTIRE PIECE WITH A LIGHT COAT OF CLEAR LACQUER.

A LARGER TEPEE CAN EASILY BE MADE BY ENLARGING THE PATTERNS WITH A TOOL CALLED THE PANTOGRAPH.

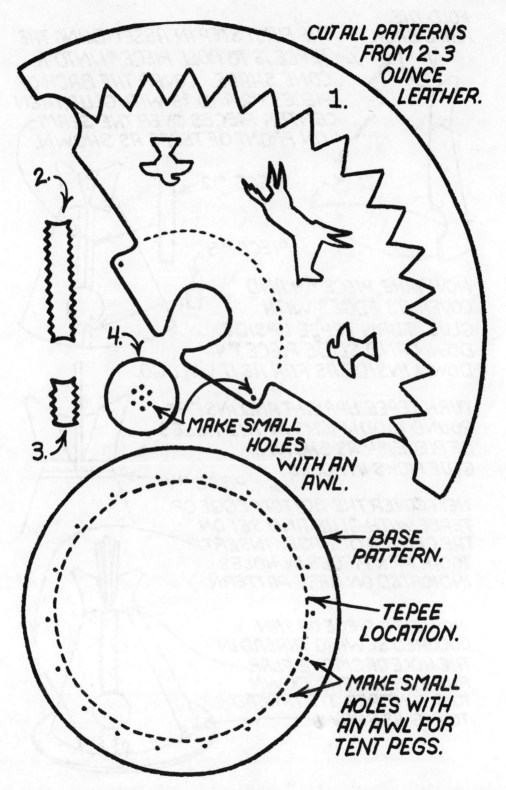

CUT ALL PATTERNS FROM 2-3 OUNCE LEATHER.

1.

2.

4.

3.

MAKE SMALL HOLES WITH AN AWL.

BASE PATTERN.

TEPEE LOCATION.

MAKE SMALL HOLES WITH AN AWL FOR TENT PEGS.

FOLD THE
FLAPS BACK.

THE FIRST STEP IN ASSEMBLING THE
TEPEE IS TO ROLL PIECE #1 INTO A
CONE SHAPE. COVER THE BACK OF
PIECES #2 AND #3 WITH GLUE, THEN
CENTER PIECES OVER THE SEAM
ON FRONT OF TEPEE AS SHOWN.

PIECE #2 →

PIECE #3 →

NOW TAKE PIECE #4 AND
COVER ITS EDGES WITH
GLUE. TURN TEPEE UPSIDE
DOWN AND SLIDE PIECE #4
DOWN INSIDE AS FAR AS IT WILL GO.

TURN TEPEE UPRIGHT AND INSERT
ROUND TOOTH PICKS IN THE HOLES
OF PIECE #4 AS SHOWN.
GLUE PICKS IN HOLES.

PIECE #4 →

NEXT COVER THE BOTTOM EDGE OF
TEPEE WITH GLUE AND SET ON
THE CENTER OF BASE. INSERT
TOOTH PICK PIECES IN HOLES
INDICATED ON BASE PATTERN.

NOW TIE A PIECE OF TAN
COLORED SEWING THREAD IN
THE HOLE OF SMOKE FLAP.
RUN THE THREAD DOWN
TO A TENT PEG. TIE THREAD
TO PEG AS SHOWN.

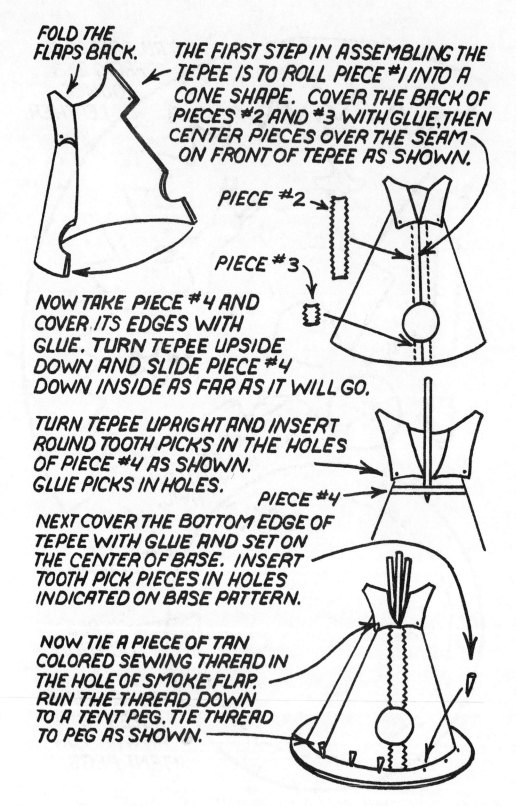

46

Wall Plaques

PATTERNS AND ASSEMBLING INSTRUCTIONS FOR THE BUTTERFLY WALL PLAQUES SHOWN BELOW ARE GIVEN ON THE FOLLOWING PAGES. IF LARGER PLAQUES ARE DESIRED, ENLARGE PATTERNS WITH A PANTOGRAPH.

ONCE THE PLAQUE HAS BEEN ASSEMBLED AS DIRECTED, SPRAY BOTH SIDES WITH SEVERAL LIGHT COATS OF BRASS OR COPPER PAINT. ALLOW PAINT TO COMPLETELY DRY BETWEEN COATS. THIS APPLICATION OF PAINT WILL HELP TO STIFFEN THE LEATHER. IF DESIRED, THE PLAQUE MAY BE LEFT NATURAL COLOR AND SPRAYED WITH CLEAR LACQUER.

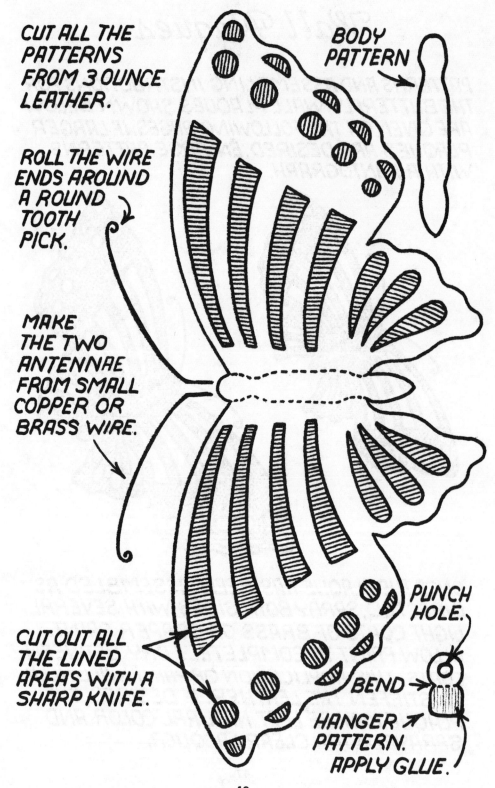

CUT ALL THE
PATTERNS
FROM 3 OUNCE
LEATHER.

BODY
PATTERN

ROLL THE WIRE
ENDS AROUND
A ROUND
TOOTH
PICK.

MAKE
THE TWO
ANTENNAE
FROM SMALL
COPPER OR
BRASS WIRE.

PUNCH
HOLE.

CUT OUT ALL
THE LINED
AREAS WITH A
SHARP KNIFE.

BEND

HANGER
PATTERN.
APPLY GLUE.

48

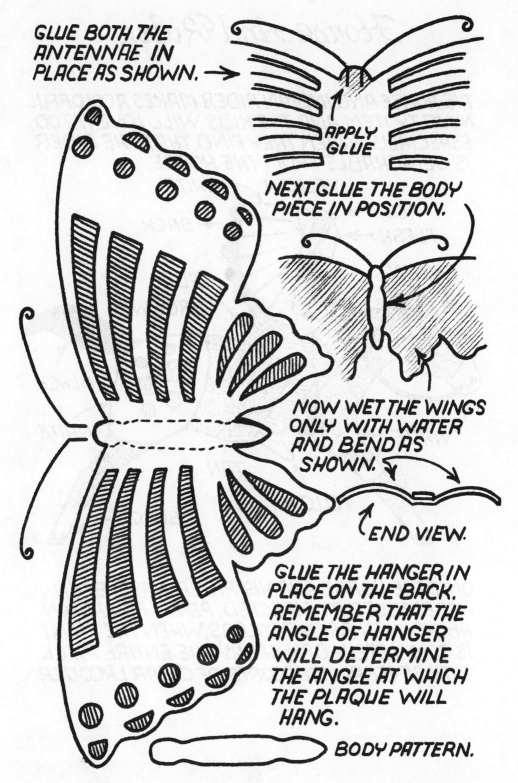

GLUE BOTH THE ANTENNAE IN PLACE AS SHOWN. →

APPLY GLUE

NEXT GLUE THE BODY PIECE IN POSITION.

NOW WET THE WINGS ONLY WITH WATER AND BEND AS SHOWN.

END VIEW.

GLUE THE HANGER IN PLACE ON THE BACK. REMEMBER THAT THE ANGLE OF HANGER WILL DETERMINE THE ANGLE AT WHICH THE PLAQUE WILL HANG.

BODY PATTERN.

Horse And Rider

THE HORSE AND INDIAN RIDER MAKES A COLORFUL NOVELTY ITEM AND THE KIDS WILL LOVE IT TOO, ESPECIALLY WHEN THEY FIND THAT THE RIDER IS DETACHABLE FROM THE HORSE.

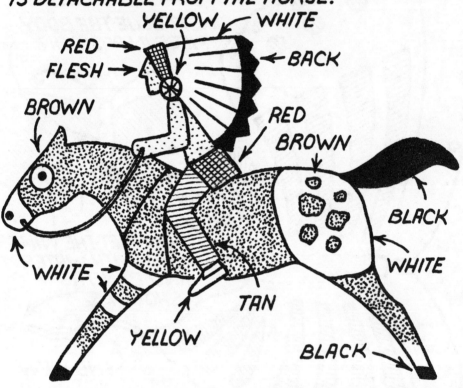

ONCE THE HORSE AND HIS RIDER HAVE BEEN ASSEMBLED AS DIRECTED, PAINT AS SHOWN ABOVE WITH BRIGHT COLORS. WHEN THE PAINT IS COMPLETELY DRY, SPRAY THE ENTIRE PIECE WITH SEVERAL LIGHT COATS OF CLEAR LACQUER.

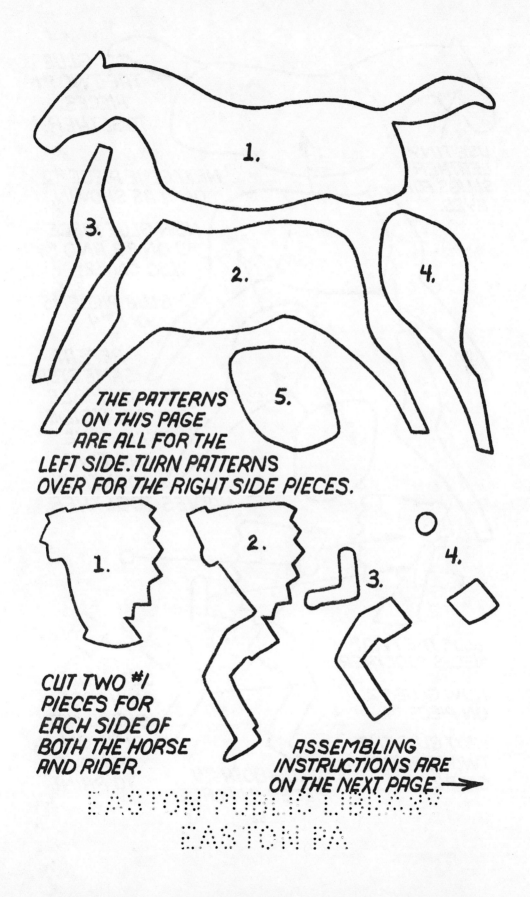

1.

3.

2.

4.

5.

THE PATTERNS
ON THIS PAGE
ARE ALL FOR THE
LEFT SIDE. TURN PATTERNS
OVER FOR THE RIGHT SIDE PIECES.

1.

2.

3.

4.

CUT TWO #1
PIECES FOR
EACH SIDE OF
BOTH THE HORSE
AND RIDER.

ASSEMBLING
INSTRUCTIONS ARE
ON THE NEXT PAGE. →

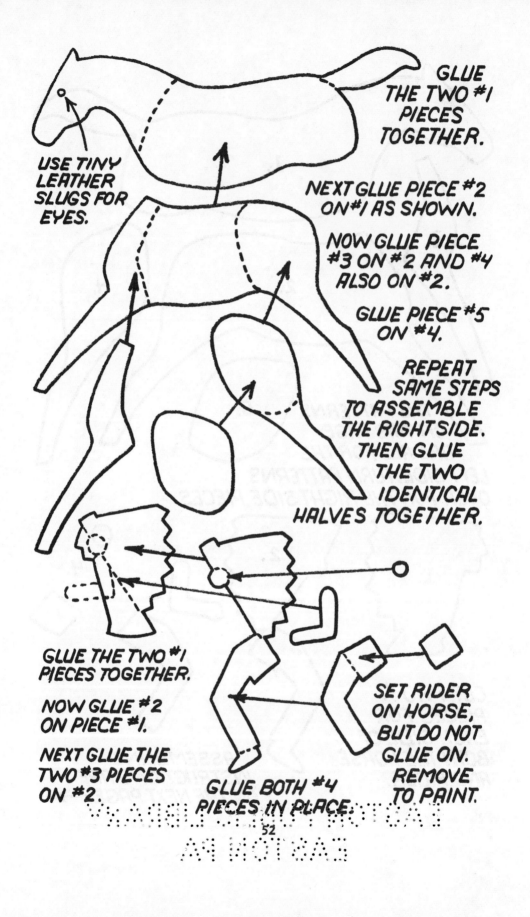

GLUE
THE TWO #1
PIECES
TOGETHER.

USE TINY
LEATHER
SLUGS FOR
EYES.

NEXT GLUE PIECE #2
ON #1 AS SHOWN.

NOW GLUE PIECE
#3 ON #2 AND #4
ALSO ON #2.

GLUE PIECE #5
ON #4.

REPEAT
SAME STEPS
TO ASSEMBLE
THE RIGHT SIDE.
THEN GLUE
THE TWO
IDENTICAL
HALVES TOGETHER.

GLUE THE TWO #1
PIECES TOGETHER.

NOW GLUE #2
ON PIECE #1.

NEXT GLUE THE
TWO #3 PIECES
ON #2.

GLUE BOTH #4
PIECES IN PLACE.

SET RIDER
ON HORSE,
BUT DO NOT
GLUE ON.
REMOVE
TO PAINT.

Glass Jackets

THESE EASY-TO-MAKE LEATHER GLASS JACKETS DRESS UP THE ORDINARY LOOKING GLASS AND NOT ONLY MAKE IT EASIER TO HOLD A COLD DRINK, BUT ALSO PROTECT THE TABLE TOPS.

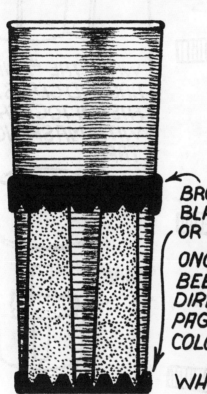

ROLLED PAPER.

BROWN, BLACK OR RED.

ONCE THE JACKET HAS BEEN ASSEMBLED AS DIRECTED ON THE NEXT PAGES, IT MAY BE COLORED IF DESIRED.

WHEN ALL THE COLORING IS FINISHED, ROLL UP A PIECE OF PAPER AND SLIDE IT DOWN INSIDE JACKET AS SHOWN. NOW SPRAY THE JACKET LIGHTLY WITH A CLEAR LACQUER. THE ROLLED PAPER WILL PREVENT THE LACQUER FROM FALLING ON THE INSIDE OF JACKET.

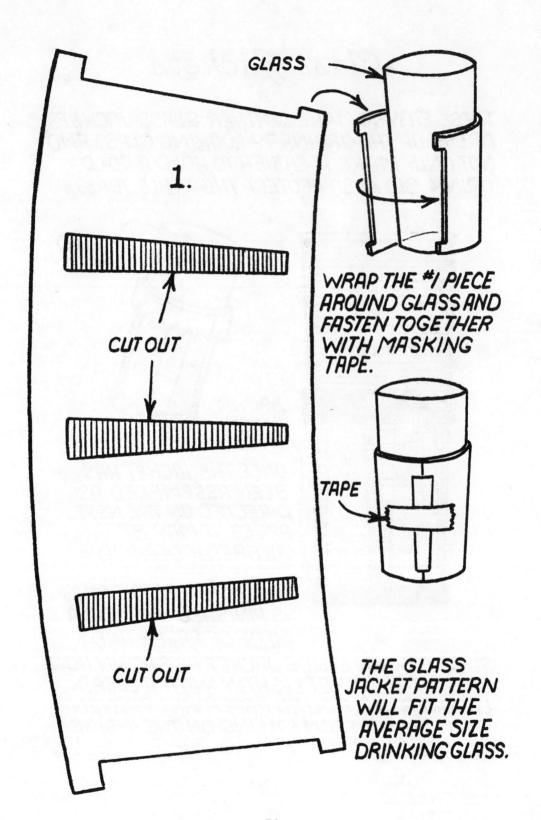

GLASS

1.

CUT OUT

CUT OUT

WRAP THE #1 PIECE AROUND GLASS AND FASTEN TOGETHER WITH MASKING TAPE.

TAPE

THE GLASS JACKET PATTERN WILL FIT THE AVERAGE SIZE DRINKING GLASS.

54

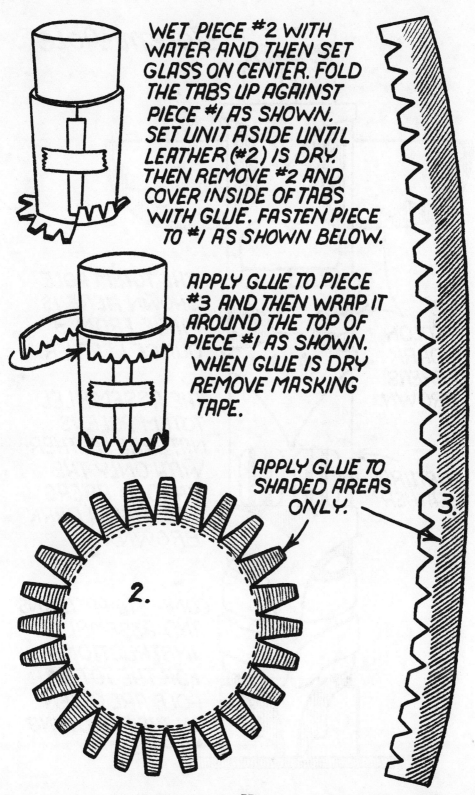

WET PIECE #2 WITH WATER AND THEN SET GLASS ON CENTER. FOLD THE TABS UP AGAINST PIECE #1 AS SHOWN. SET UNIT ASIDE UNTIL LEATHER (#2) IS DRY. THEN REMOVE #2 AND COVER INSIDE OF TABS WITH GLUE. FASTEN PIECE TO #1 AS SHOWN BELOW.

APPLY GLUE TO PIECE #3 AND THEN WRAP IT AROUND THE TOP OF PIECE #1 AS SHOWN. WHEN GLUE IS DRY REMOVE MASKING TAPE.

APPLY GLUE TO SHADED AREAS ONLY.

3.

2.

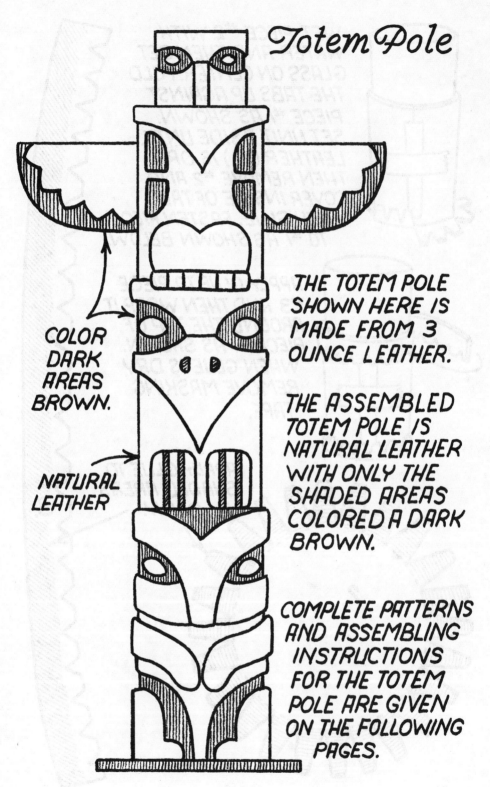

TotemPole

COLOR
DARK
AREAS
BROWN.

NATURAL
LEATHER

THE TOTEM POLE
SHOWN HERE IS
MADE FROM 3
OUNCE LEATHER.

THE ASSEMBLED
TOTEM POLE IS
NATURAL LEATHER
WITH ONLY THE
SHADED AREAS
COLORED A DARK
BROWN.

COMPLETE PATTERNS
AND ASSEMBLING
INSTRUCTIONS
FOR THE TOTEM
POLE ARE GIVEN
ON THE FOLLOWING
PAGES.

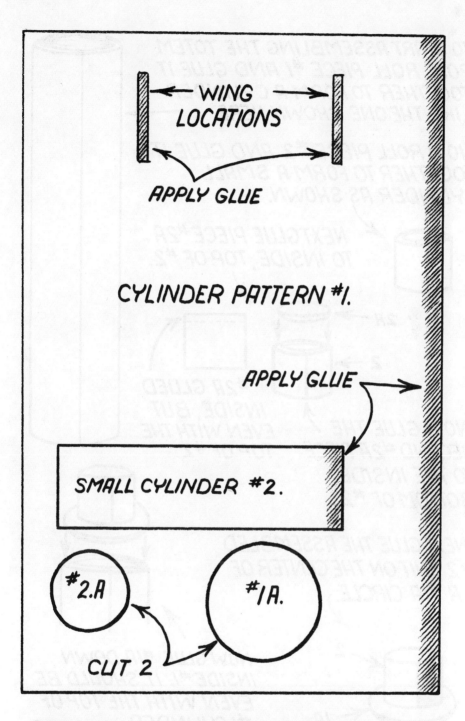

WING LOCATIONS

APPLY GLUE

CYLINDER PATTERN #1.

APPLY GLUE

SMALL CYLINDER #2.

#2.A

#1A.

CUT 2

APPLY GLUE TO THE PATTERNS SHOWN ON THIS PAGE ONLY WHERE INDICATED.

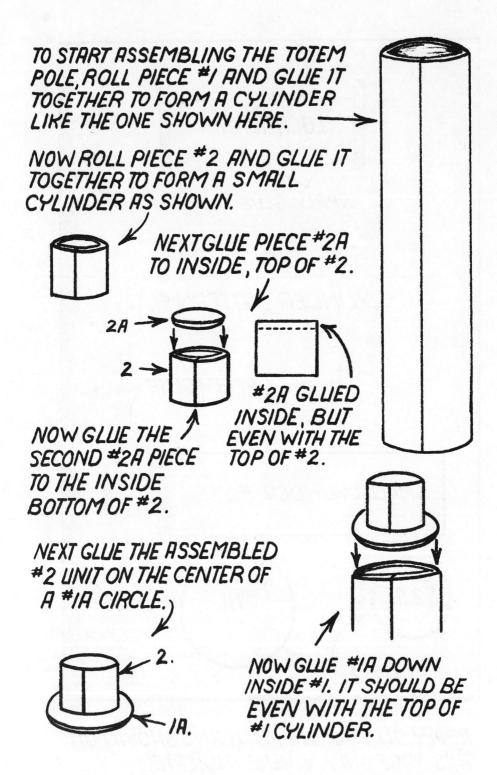

TO START ASSEMBLING THE TOTEM POLE, ROLL PIECE #1 AND GLUE IT TOGETHER TO FORM A CYLINDER LIKE THE ONE SHOWN HERE.

NOW ROLL PIECE #2 AND GLUE IT TOGETHER TO FORM A SMALL CYLINDER AS SHOWN.

NEXT GLUE PIECE #2A TO INSIDE, TOP OF #2.

2A

2

#2A GLUED INSIDE, BUT EVEN WITH THE TOP OF #2.

NOW GLUE THE SECOND #2A PIECE TO THE INSIDE BOTTOM OF #2.

NEXT GLUE THE ASSEMBLED #2 UNIT ON THE CENTER OF A #1A CIRCLE.

2.

1A.

NOW GLUE #1A DOWN INSIDE #1. IT SHOULD BE EVEN WITH THE TOP OF #1 CYLINDER.

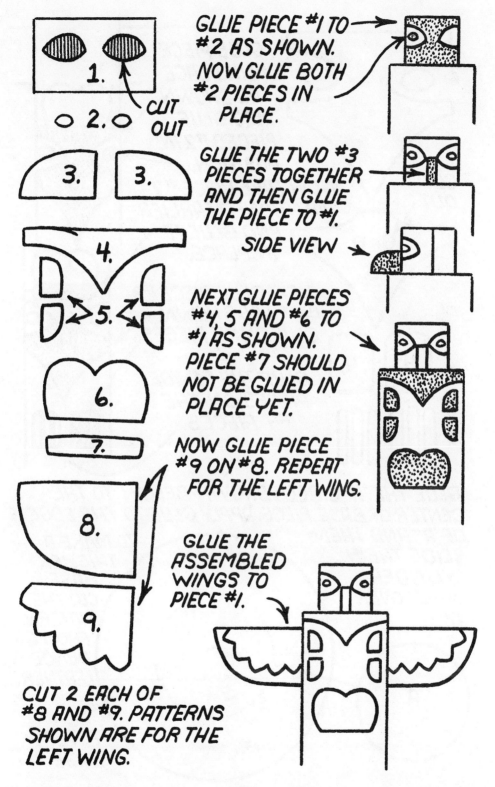

1.

CUT OUT

2.

GLUE PIECE #1 TO #2 AS SHOWN. NOW GLUE BOTH #2 PIECES IN PLACE.

3. 3.

GLUE THE TWO #3 PIECES TOGETHER AND THEN GLUE THE PIECE TO #1.

SIDE VIEW

4.

5.

6.

NEXT GLUE PIECES #4, 5 AND #6 TO #1 AS SHOWN. PIECE #7 SHOULD NOT BE GLUED IN PLACE YET.

7.

NOW GLUE PIECE #9 ON #8. REPEAT FOR THE LEFT WING.

8.

9.

GLUE THE ASSEMBLED WINGS TO PIECE #1.

CUT 2 EACH OF #8 AND #9. PATTERNS SHOWN ARE FOR THE LEFT WING.

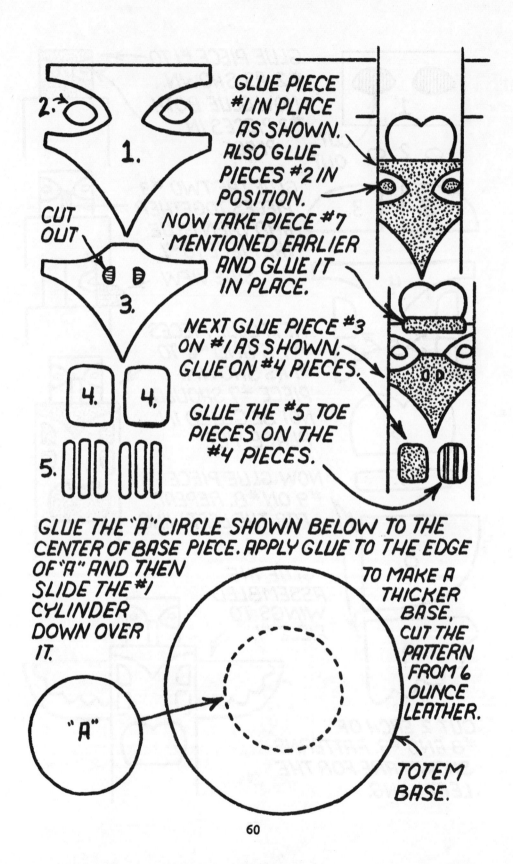

GLUE PIECE #1 IN PLACE AS SHOWN. ALSO GLUE PIECES #2 IN POSITION.

NOW TAKE PIECE #7 MENTIONED EARLIER AND GLUE IT IN PLACE.

NEXT GLUE PIECE #3 ON #1 AS SHOWN. GLUE ON #4 PIECES.

GLUE THE #5 TOE PIECES ON THE #4 PIECES.

1.

2.

CUT OUT

3.

4. 4.

5.

GLUE THE "A" CIRCLE SHOWN BELOW TO THE CENTER OF BASE PIECE. APPLY GLUE TO THE EDGE OF "A" AND THEN SLIDE THE #1 CYLINDER DOWN OVER IT.

TO MAKE A THICKER BASE, CUT THE PATTERN FROM 6 OUNCE LEATHER.

"A"

TOTEM BASE.

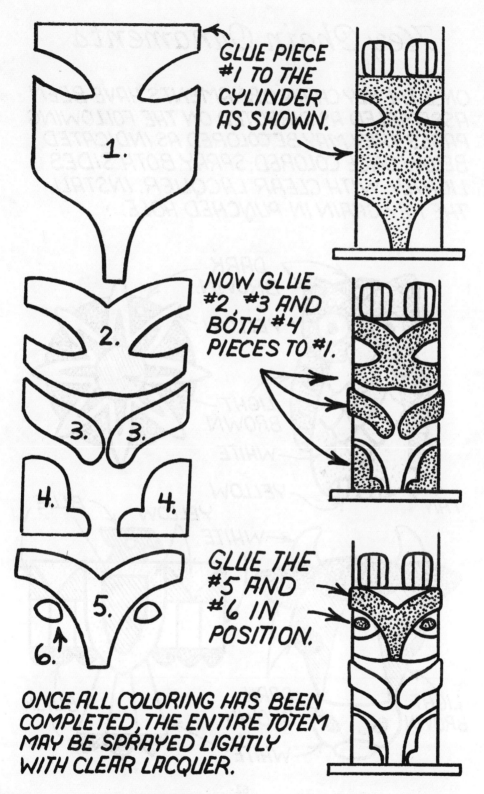

GLUE PIECE #1 TO THE CYLINDER AS SHOWN.

NOW GLUE #2, #3 AND BOTH #4 PIECES TO #1.

GLUE THE #5 AND #6 IN POSITION.

ONCE ALL COLORING HAS BEEN COMPLETED, THE ENTIRE TOTEM MAY BE SPRAYED LIGHTLY WITH CLEAR LACQUER.

Key Chain Ornaments

ONCE THE KEY CHAIN ORNAMENTS HAVE BEEN ASSEMBLED AS DIRECTED ON THE FOLLOWING PAGES, THEY MAY BE COLORED AS INDICATED BELOW. ONCE COLORED, SPRAY BOTH SIDES LIGHTLY WITH CLEAR LACQUER. INSTALL THE KEY CHAIN IN PUNCHED HOLE.

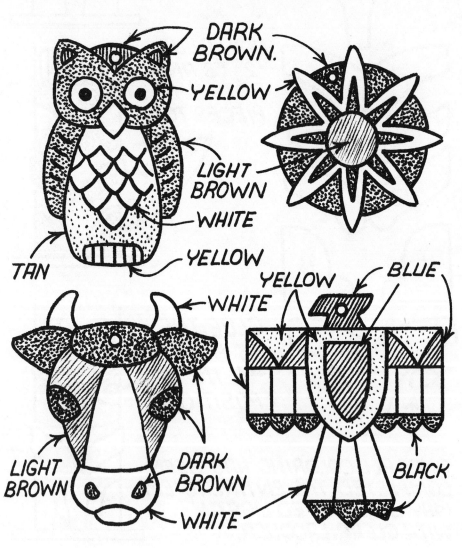

DARK BROWN.

YELLOW

LIGHT BROWN

WHITE

YELLOW

TAN

WHITE

YELLOW

BLUE

LIGHT BROWN

DARK BROWN

WHITE

BLACK

PUNCH HOLE

1.

THIS ORNAMENT WILL APPEAR THE SAME ON BOTH SIDES SO IT WILL BE REQUIRED TO CUT OUT 2 OF EACH PATTERN. BE SURE TO TURN THESE PATTERNS OVER FOR OPPOSITE SIDE PIECES.

CUT OUT

2.

TO ASSEMBLE, GLUE PIECE #2 ON #1 AS SHOWN.

NOW GLUE PIECE #3 TO CENTER OF PIECE #2.

3.

FOLLOW THESE SAME ASSEMBLY STEPS FOR THE OPPOSITE SIDE.

INSTALL KEY CHAIN IN THE PUNCHED HOLE.

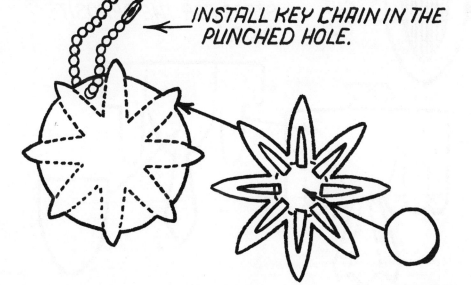

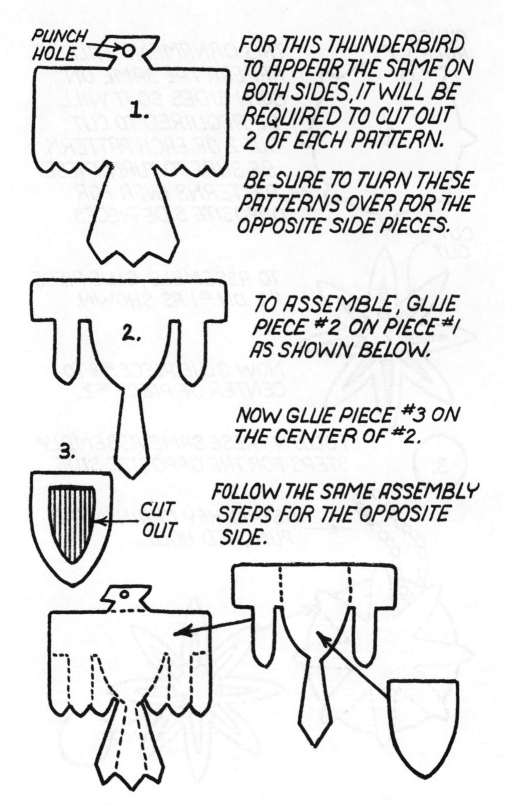

PUNCH HOLE

1.

FOR THIS THUNDERBIRD TO APPEAR THE SAME ON BOTH SIDES, IT WILL BE REQUIRED TO CUT OUT 2 OF EACH PATTERN.

BE SURE TO TURN THESE PATTERNS OVER FOR THE OPPOSITE SIDE PIECES.

2.

TO ASSEMBLE, GLUE PIECE #2 ON PIECE #1 AS SHOWN BELOW.

NOW GLUE PIECE #3 ON THE CENTER OF #2.

3.

CUT OUT

FOLLOW THE SAME ASSEMBLY STEPS FOR THE OPPOSITE SIDE.

64

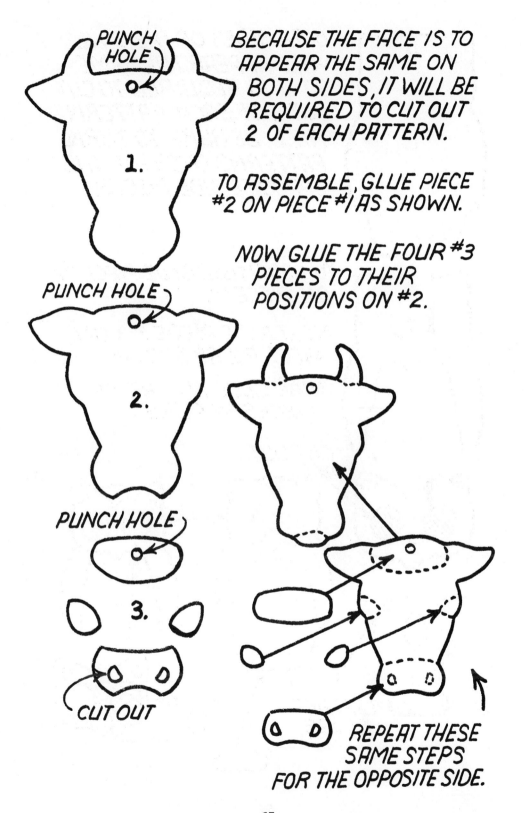

PUNCH HOLE

1.

BECAUSE THE FACE IS TO
APPEAR THE SAME ON
BOTH SIDES, IT WILL BE
REQUIRED TO CUT OUT
2 OF EACH PATTERN.

TO ASSEMBLE, GLUE PIECE
#2 ON PIECE #1 AS SHOWN.

NOW GLUE THE FOUR #3
PIECES TO THEIR
POSITIONS ON #2.

PUNCH HOLE

2.

PUNCH HOLE

3.

CUT OUT

REPEAT THESE
SAME STEPS
FOR THE OPPOSITE SIDE.

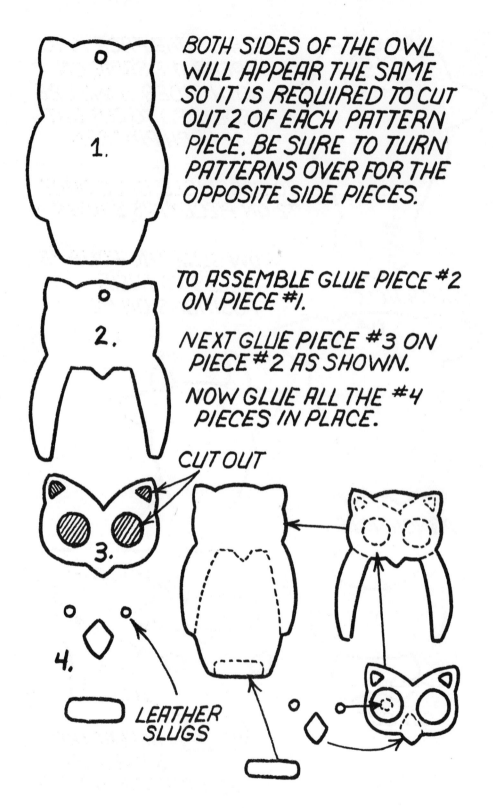

1.

BOTH SIDES OF THE OWL
WILL APPEAR THE SAME
SO IT IS REQUIRED TO CUT
OUT 2 OF EACH PATTERN
PIECE. BE SURE TO TURN
PATTERNS OVER FOR THE
OPPOSITE SIDE PIECES.

2.

TO ASSEMBLE GLUE PIECE #2
ON PIECE #1.

NEXT GLUE PIECE #3 ON
PIECE #2 AS SHOWN.

NOW GLUE ALL THE #4
PIECES IN PLACE.

CUT OUT

3.

4.

LEATHER
SLUGS

Wise Owl

COMPLETE PATTERNS AND INSTRUCTIONS FOR CONSTRUCTING THE WISE OWL ARE GIVEN ON THE FOLLOWING PAGES.

ONCE THE WISE OWL HAS BEEN ASSEMBLED AS DIRECTED, HE MAY BE COLORED. PIECE #2 IS COLORED A MEDIUM BROWN, THE EXPOSED INSIDE PARTS ARE COLORED A DARK BROWN. PIECE #1 IS A LIGHT TAN, EXCEPT FOR THE CENTER SECTION, WHICH IS COLORED WHITE. THE FEATHERS ON THE WHITE CHEST AREA ARE OUTLINED WITH A MEDIUM BROWN. THE LARGE EYES ARE COLORED YELLOW WITH THE CENTER BLACK. COLOR THE TOOTH PICK LEGS TAN AND THE FEET A MEDIUM BROWN.

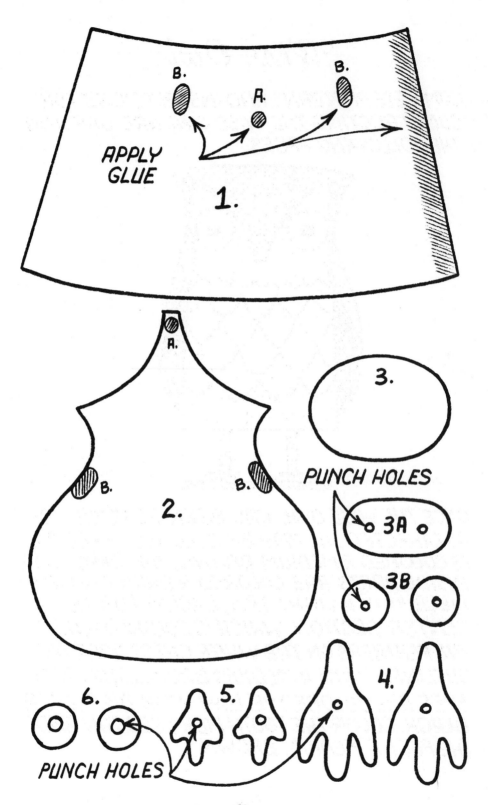

APPLY GLUE

1.

B.

A.

B.

A.

2.

B.

B.

3.

PUNCH HOLES

3A

3B

4.

5.

6.

PUNCH HOLES

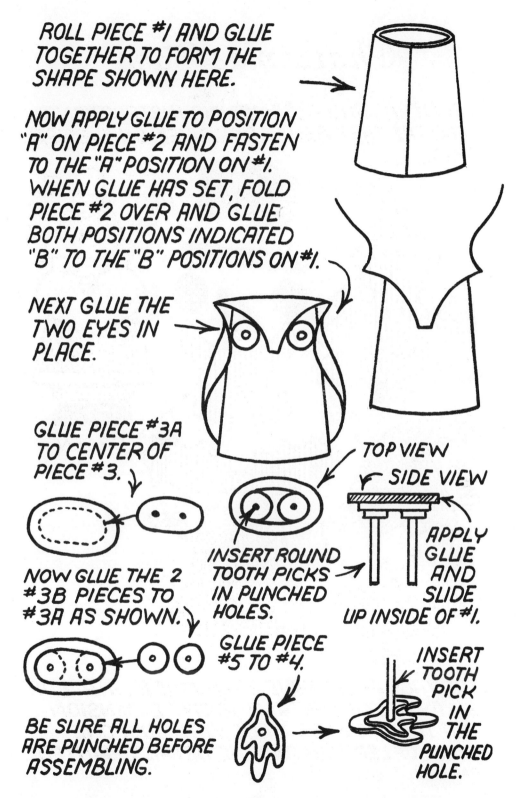

ROLL PIECE #1 AND GLUE TOGETHER TO FORM THE SHAPE SHOWN HERE.

NOW APPLY GLUE TO POSITION "A" ON PIECE #2 AND FASTEN TO THE "A" POSITION ON #1. WHEN GLUE HAS SET, FOLD PIECE #2 OVER AND GLUE BOTH POSITIONS INDICATED "B" TO THE "B" POSITIONS ON #1.

NEXT GLUE THE TWO EYES IN PLACE.

GLUE PIECE #3A TO CENTER OF PIECE #3.

TOP VIEW

SIDE VIEW

APPLY GLUE AND SLIDE UP INSIDE OF #1.

INSERT ROUND TOOTH PICKS IN PUNCHED HOLES.

NOW GLUE THE 2 #3B PIECES TO #3A AS SHOWN.

GLUE PIECE #5 TO #4.

INSERT TOOTH PICK IN THE PUNCHED HOLE.

BE SURE ALL HOLES ARE PUNCHED BEFORE ASSEMBLING.

69

Christmas Tags

PATTERNS AND ASSEMBLING INSTRUCTIONS FOR THE TAGS BELOW ARE GIVEN ON THE NEXT PAGE.

THE TAGS ABOVE HAVE BEEN MADE WITH 2 OR 3 LAYERS OF LEATHER TO GIVE DIMENSION, BUT THEY MAY BE MADE WITH JUST ONE PIECE OF LEATHER AND THE DETAILS PAINTED ON.

THE PIECES ARE GLUED ONE ON
TOP OF THE OTHER, JUST AS WITH
THE LEATHER ANIMALS.

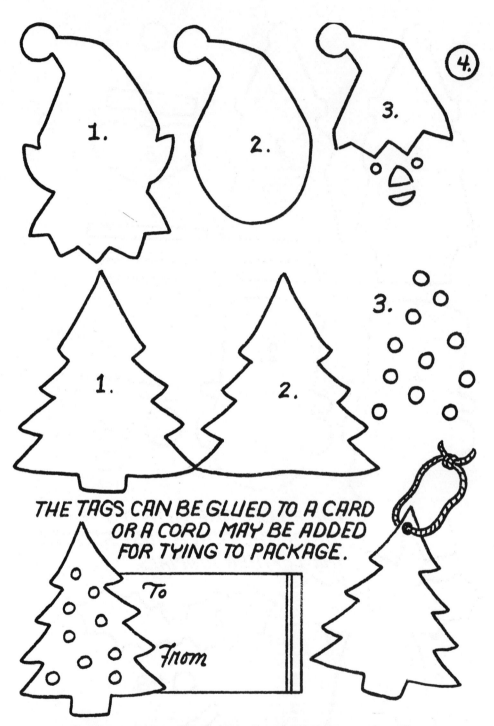

THE TAGS CAN BE GLUED TO A CARD OR A CORD MAY BE ADDED FOR TYING TO PACKAGE.

To

From

BY ENLARGING PATTERNS SLIGHTLY AND COLORING BOTH SIDES, THESE SAME TAGS MAY BE HUNG ON THE CHRISTMAS TREE.

Leather Wiseman

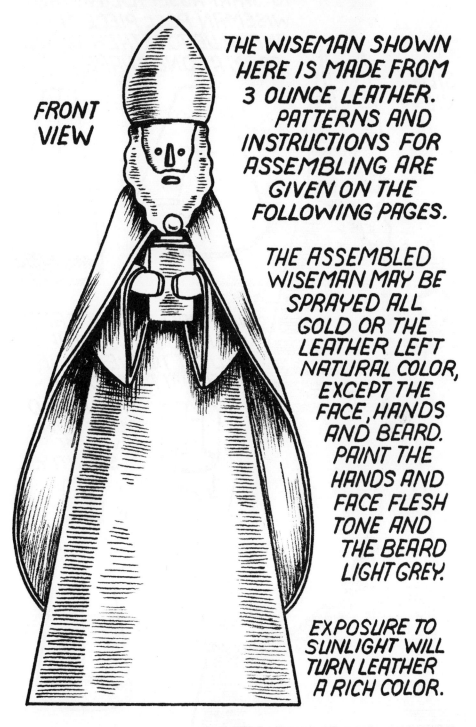

FRONT VIEW

THE WISEMAN SHOWN HERE IS MADE FROM 3 OUNCE LEATHER. PATTERNS AND INSTRUCTIONS FOR ASSEMBLING ARE GIVEN ON THE FOLLOWING PAGES.

THE ASSEMBLED WISEMAN MAY BE SPRAYED ALL GOLD OR THE LEATHER LEFT NATURAL COLOR, EXCEPT THE FACE, HANDS AND BEARD. PAINT THE HANDS AND FACE FLESH TONE AND THE BEARD LIGHT GREY.

EXPOSURE TO SUNLIGHT WILL TURN LEATHER A RICH COLOR.

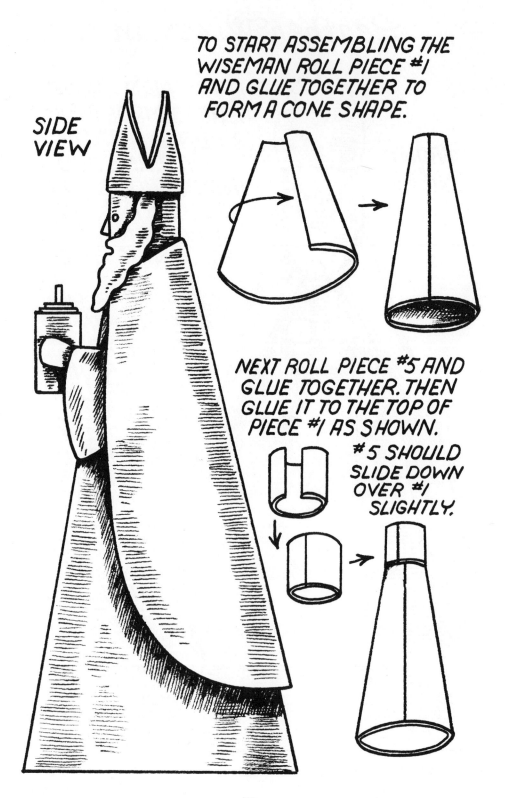

SIDE VIEW

TO START ASSEMBLING THE WISEMAN ROLL PIECE #1 AND GLUE TOGETHER TO FORM A CONE SHAPE.

NEXT ROLL PIECE #5 AND GLUE TOGETHER. THEN GLUE IT TO THE TOP OF PIECE #1 AS SHOWN.

#5 SHOULD SLIDE DOWN OVER #1 SLIGHTLY.

FOLD PIECE #3 WHERE INDICATED AND GLUE TOGETHER AS SHOWN.

APPLY GLUE

NOW GLUE BOTH THE #3 PIECES TO THEIR CORRECT LOCATIONS ON #1.

GLUE

BE SURE BOTH ARMS ARE IN THEIR CORRECT LOCATION.

NEXT WRAP PIECE #2 AROUND FIGURE AND GLUE IN PLACE.

APPLY GLUE ONLY WHERE INDICATED ON PATTERN.

FOLD PIECE #4 AS DIRECTED AND GLUE TOGETHER. NOW GLUE IT TO THE TOP OF #5 AS SHOW BELOW.

#4 SHOULD SLIDE DOWN OVER #5 SLIGHTLY.

GLUE TAB TO INSIDE.

GLUE THE EYES AND NOSE TO FACE.

GLUE BEARD TO PIECE #5.

GLUE HANDS TO INSIDE OF SLEEVES.

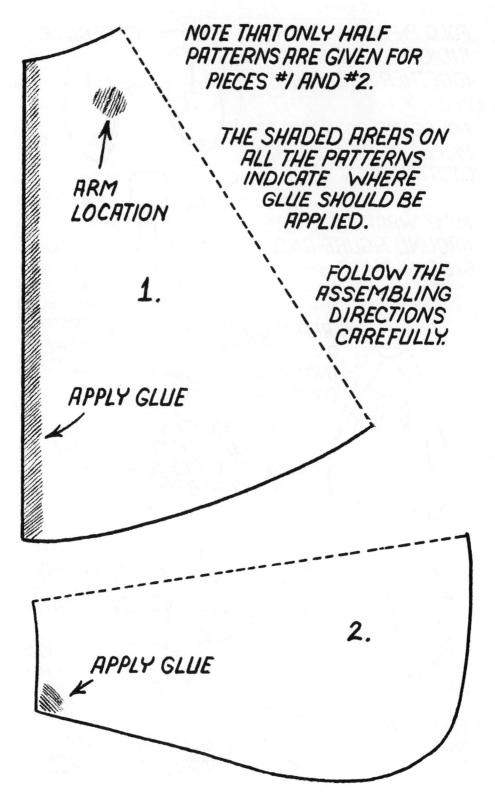

NOTE THAT ONLY HALF PATTERNS ARE GIVEN FOR PIECES #1 AND #2.

THE SHADED AREAS ON ALL THE PATTERNS INDICATE WHERE GLUE SHOULD BE APPLIED.

FOLLOW THE ASSEMBLING DIRECTIONS CAREFULLY.

ARM LOCATION

1.

APPLY GLUE

2.

APPLY GLUE

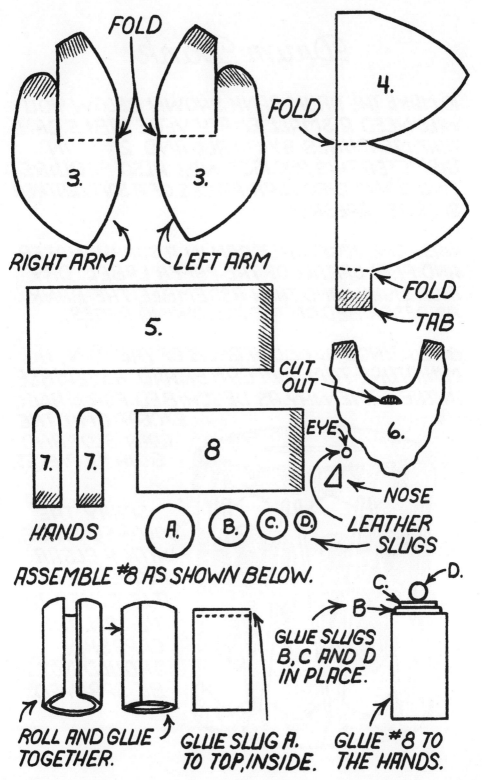

FOLD

FOLD

4.

RIGHT ARM   LEFT ARM

3.   3.

FOLD

TAB

5.

CUT OUT

8

EYE

6.

7.   7.

NOSE

A.   B.   C.   D.

LEATHER SLUGS

HANDS

ASSEMBLE #8 AS SHOWN BELOW.

C.   D.

B

GLUE SLUGS B, C AND D IN PLACE.

ROLL AND GLUE TOGETHER.

GLUE SLUG A. TO TOP, INSIDE.

GLUE #8 TO THE HANDS.

77

Drum Bank

TO MAKE THE DRUM BANK SHOWN BELOW YOU WILL NEED A SMALL, EMPTY VEGETABLE CAN THAT MEASURES 3 1/4" TALL AND 2 3/4" IN DIAMETER. THIS PROJECT WILL ALSO REQUIRE TWO 3 3/4" CIRCULAR PIECES OF A SOFT LEATHER SUCH AS CAPESKIN.

WASH THE VEGETABLE CAN IN A SOAPY WATER AND PEEL OFF ALL OF THE PAPER LABEL. DRY THOROUGHLY, AND THEN ASSEMBLE THE BANK AS DESCRIBED ON THE FOLLOWING PAGES.

BY CUTTINGS OUT BOTH ENDS OF THE CAN, A MINIATURE TOM TOM CAN BE HAD. ASSEMBLE IN THE SAME WAY AS DESCRIBED FOR BANK, EXCEPT OMIT THE COIN SLOT AND BOTH #2 PIECES.

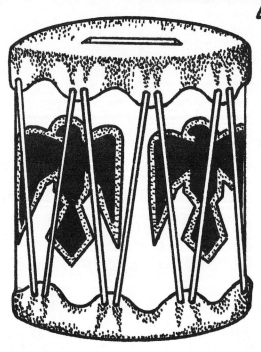

SPRAY THE COLORED PIECE WITH A CLEAR LACQUER BEFORE IT IS GLUED TO THE CAN. THE CAPESKIN SHOULD NOT BE SPRAYED.

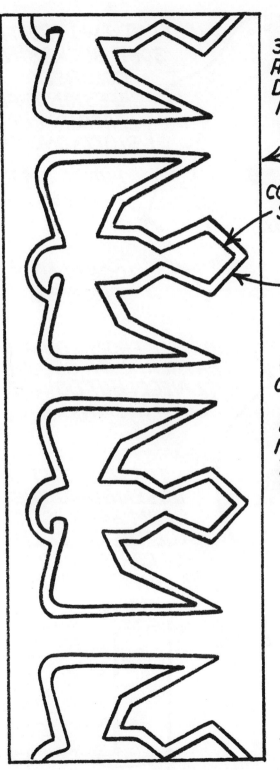

CUT PIECE FROM 3 OUNCE LEATHER AND PAINT THE DESIGNS BEFORE IT IS GLUED ON THE CAN.

COLOR THUNDERBIRD SOLID BLACK AND THE OUTLINE AROUND IT A BRIGHT RED OR BLUE.

CUT BOTH ENDS OF THE PATTERN AS STRAIGHT AS POSSIBLE FOR A NEAT JOINT WHEN THE PIECE IS GLUED ON THE CAN.

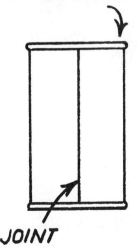

JOINT

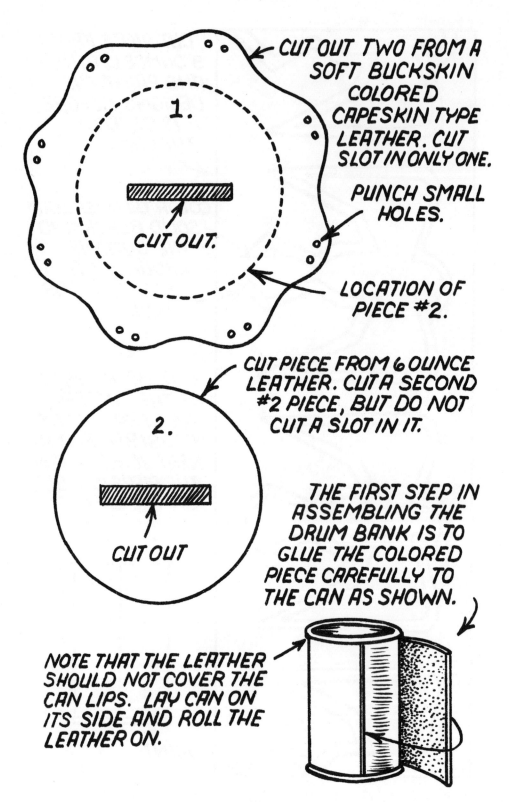

CUT OUT TWO FROM A SOFT BUCKSKIN COLORED CAPESKIN TYPE LEATHER. CUT SLOT IN ONLY ONE.

1.

CUT OUT.

PUNCH SMALL HOLES.

LOCATION OF PIECE #2.

CUT PIECE FROM 6 OUNCE LEATHER. CUT A SECOND #2 PIECE, BUT DO NOT CUT A SLOT IN IT.

2.

CUT OUT

THE FIRST STEP IN ASSEMBLING THE DRUM BANK IS TO GLUE THE COLORED PIECE CAREFULLY TO THE CAN AS SHOWN.

NOTE THAT THE LEATHER SHOULD NOT COVER THE CAN LIPS. LAY CAN ON ITS SIDE AND ROLL THE LEATHER ON.

80

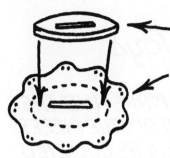

NEXT GLUE THE SLOTTED #2 PIECE TO THE CENTER OF THE SLOTTED #1 PIECE. BE SURE THE SLOTS IN BOTH PIECES LINE UP. NOW GLUE THE REMAINING #2 PIECE TO THE CENTER OF THE SECOND #1 PIECE.

NOW COVER PIECE #2 (WITHOUT THE SLOT) WITH GLUE AND SET ON BOTTOM OF CAN. SET TO ONE SIDE UNTIL GLUE IS DRY. NOTE THAT #2 SETS DOWN INSIDE THE CAN LIP, GIVING THE CAN A SOLID-FEELING BOTTOM.

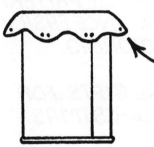

CAN WITH #1 AND #2 PIECES IN PLACE ON BOTTOM OF THE CAN.

NEXT TURN THE CAN OVER AND SET PIECE #1 AND #2 (BOTH SLOTTED) ON TOP OF THE CAN. NOTE AGAIN THAT PIECE #2 SETS DOWN INSIDE CAN.

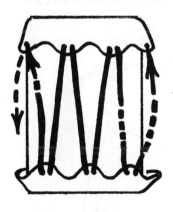

NOW WITH A PIECE OF HEAVY CORD, LACE THE TOP #1 PIECE TO THE BOTTOM #1, PIECE AS SHOWN. TIE THE CORD IN A SIMPLE KNOT AS THE CORD MUST BE UNLACED TO EMPTY THE CONTENTS OF THE BANK.

Clothespin Toys

CLOTHESPIN TOYS ARE EASY TO MAKE AND THE KIDS JUST LOVE THEM. CUT OUT ALL THE PIECES FOR EACH FIGURE AND ASSEMBLE AS DIRECTED. COLOR THE CLOTHESPINS TO MATCH THE FIGURE. SPRAY THE FINISHED FIGURES WITH SEVERAL LIGHT COATS OF CLEAR LACQUER.

ONCE YOU HAVE COMPLETED THE HORSE AND COWBOY YOU MAY WISH TO MAKE MORE CLOTHESPIN TOYS, SO ADDITIONAL FIGURES HAVE BEEN GIVEN. THE SAME HORSE PATTERN MAY BE USED AND HIS APPEARANCE EASILY CHANGED WITH DIFFERENT COLORING.

CLOTHESPIN TOYS MAKE IDEAL GIFTS FOR CHILDREN. MAKE SOME FOR CHRISTMAS.

THE ASSEMBLED COWBOY AND HORSE.

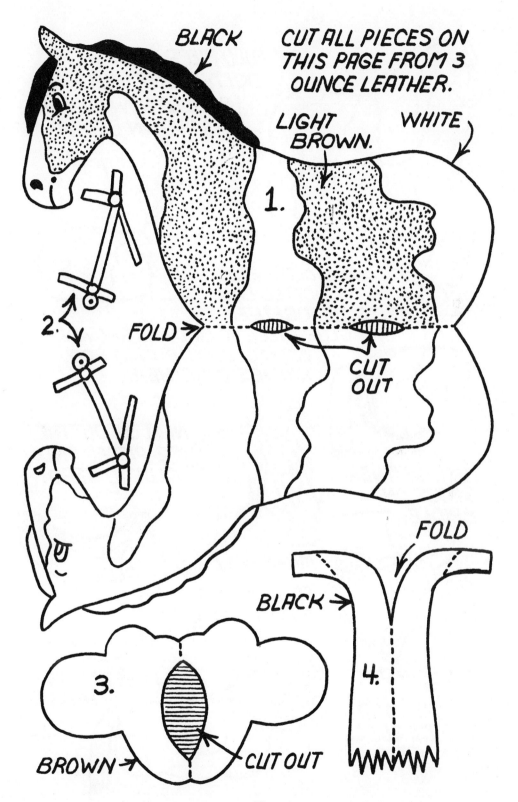

BLACK

CUT ALL PIECES ON THIS PAGE FROM 3 OUNCE LEATHER.

LIGHT BROWN.

WHITE

1.

2.

FOLD

CUT OUT

FOLD

BLACK →

4.

3.

BROWN →

CUT OUT

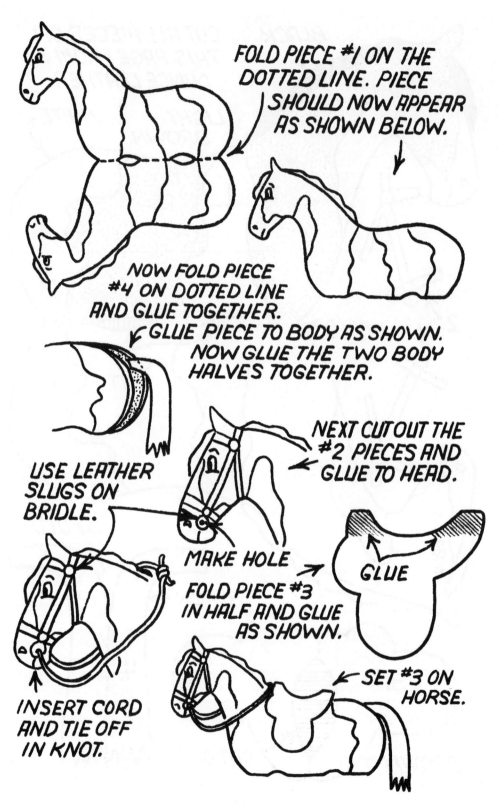

FOLD PIECE #1 ON THE DOTTED LINE. PIECE SHOULD NOW APPEAR AS SHOWN BELOW.

NOW FOLD PIECE #4 ON DOTTED LINE AND GLUE TOGETHER.

GLUE PIECE TO BODY AS SHOWN. NOW GLUE THE TWO BODY HALVES TOGETHER.

USE LEATHER SLUGS ON BRIDLE.

NEXT CUT OUT THE #2 PIECES AND GLUE TO HEAD.

MAKE HOLE

GLUE

FOLD PIECE #3 IN HALF AND GLUE AS SHOWN.

INSERT CORD AND TIE OFF IN KNOT.

SET #3 ON HORSE.

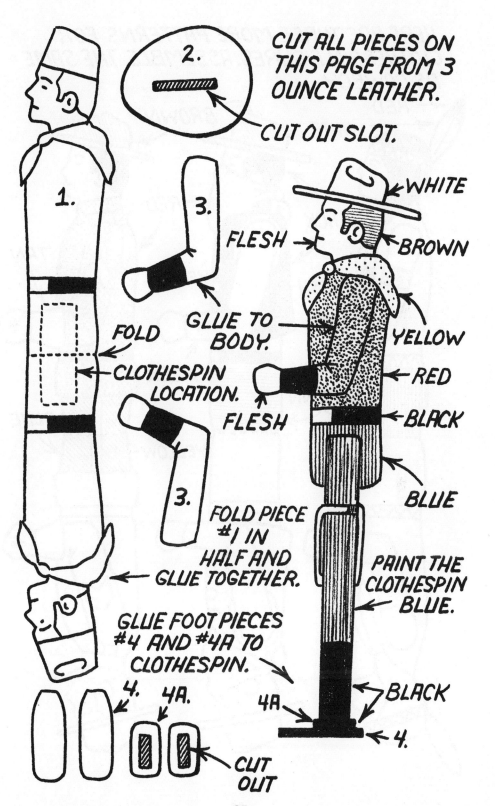

2.

CUT ALL PIECES ON THIS PAGE FROM 3 OUNCE LEATHER.

CUT OUT SLOT.

1.

3.

FLESH

WHITE

BROWN

GLUE TO BODY.

YELLOW

FOLD

RED

CLOTHESPIN LOCATION.

FLESH

BLACK

3.

BLUE

FOLD PIECE #1 IN HALF AND GLUE TOGETHER.

PAINT THE CLOTHESPIN BLUE.

GLUE FOOT PIECES #4 AND #4A TO CLOTHESPIN.

4. 4A.

4A

BLACK

CUT OUT

4.

HERE ARE THREE MORE PATTERNS FOR CLOTHESPIN FIGURES. ASSEMBLE THE SAME AS COWBOY.

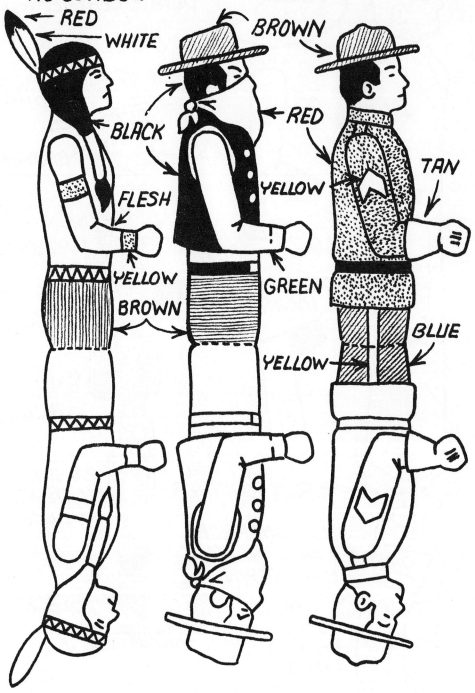

RED
WHITE
BROWN
BLACK
RED
TAN
FLESH
YELLOW
YELLOW
GREEN
BROWN
BLUE
YELLOW

Leather Flowers

WITH THE PATTERN GIVEN BELOW, CONSTRUCT SEVERAL OR MORE LEATHER DAISIES AND THEN MAKE A COLORFUL AND UNUSUAL FLOWER ARRANGEMENT FOR YOUR TABLE. CUT PIECE #1 FROM 3 OUNCE LEATHER AND PIECE #2 FROM 4-5 OUNCE LEATHER. ASSEMBLE AS SHOWN, COLOR AND THEN SPRAY LIGHTLY WITH CLEAR LACQUER.

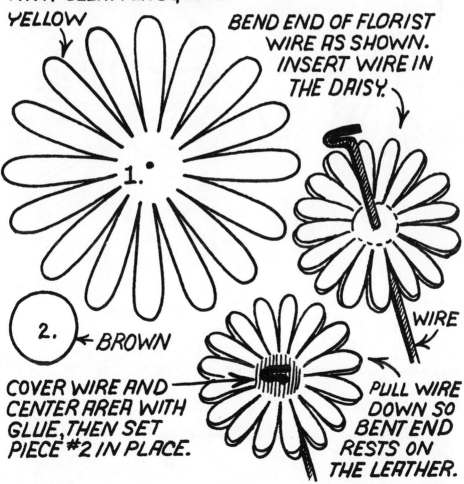

YELLOW

BEND END OF FLORIST WIRE AS SHOWN. INSERT WIRE IN THE DAISY.

1.

2. ← BROWN

WIRE

COVER WIRE AND CENTER AREA WITH GLUE, THEN SET PIECE #2 IN PLACE.

PULL WIRE DOWN SO BENT END RESTS ON THE LEATHER.

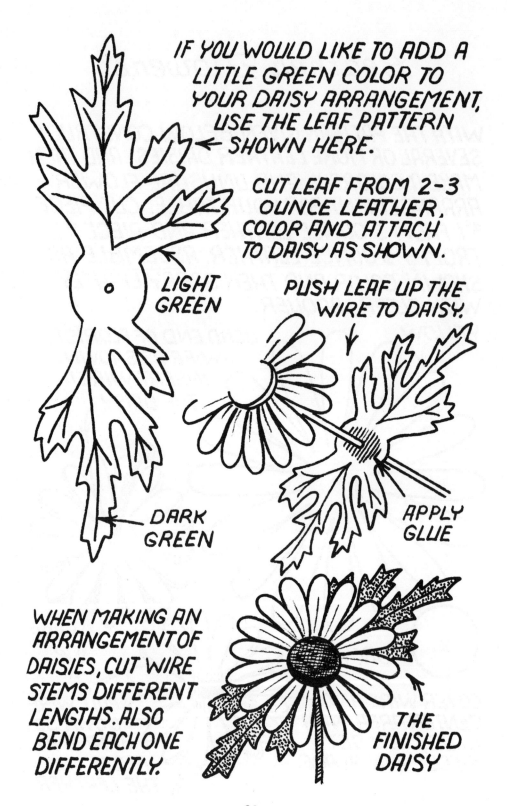

IF YOU WOULD LIKE TO ADD A LITTLE GREEN COLOR TO YOUR DAISY ARRANGEMENT, USE THE LEAF PATTERN SHOWN HERE.

CUT LEAF FROM 2-3 OUNCE LEATHER, COLOR AND ATTACH TO DAISY AS SHOWN.

LIGHT GREEN

PUSH LEAF UP THE WIRE TO DAISY.

DARK GREEN

APPLY GLUE

WHEN MAKING AN ARRANGEMENT OF DAISIES, CUT WIRE STEMS DIFFERENT LENGTHS. ALSO BEND EACH ONE DIFFERENTLY.

THE FINISHED DAISY

Earrings

CUT THE EARRINGS SHOWN BELOW FROM 3 - 5 OUNCE LEATHER. ASSEMBLE AS DIRECTED, COLOR AND THEN SPRAY THE SURFACE WITH SEVERAL LIGHT COATS OF CLEAR LACQUER. GLUE EARRING BACKS IN PLACE.

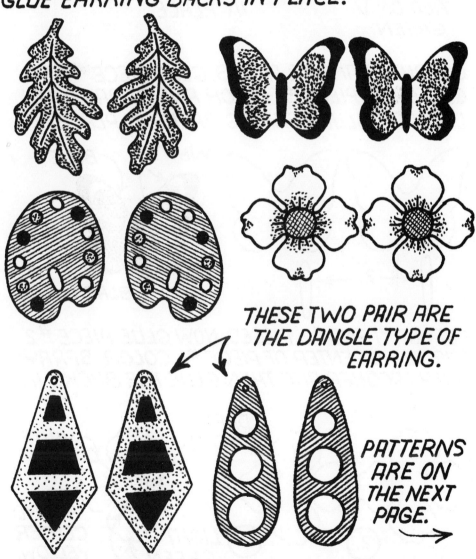

THESE TWO PAIR ARE THE DANGLE TYPE OF EARRING.

PATTERNS ARE ON THE NEXT PAGE. →

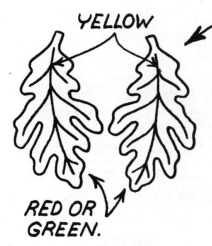

YELLOW

RED OR GREEN.

THESE EARRINGS ARE MADE FROM ONE PIECE OF LEATHER. CUT OUT, COLOR RED OR GREEN WITH VEINS YELLOW. SPRAY WITH LACQUER THEN GLUE THE BACKS IN PLACE.

CUT OUT #1 AND #2 PIECES. GLUE PIECE #2 ON CENTER OF PIECE #1. COLOR AND SPRAY WITH LACQUER. GLUE EARRING BACKS IN PLACE.

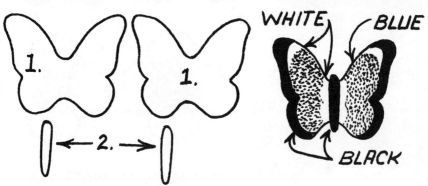

1.

1.

←— 2. —→

WHITE

BLUE

BLACK

CUT OUT #1 AND #2 PIECES. NOW GLUE PIECE #2 (CIRCLE) TO CENTER OF PIECE #1. COLOR, SPRAY WITH LACQUER AND THEN GLUE THE BACKS IN PLACE.

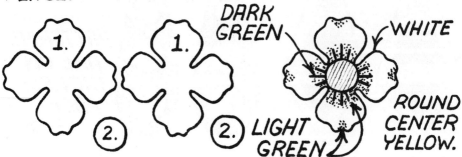

1.

1.

2.

2.

DARK GREEN

WHITE

LIGHT GREEN

ROUND CENTER YELLOW.

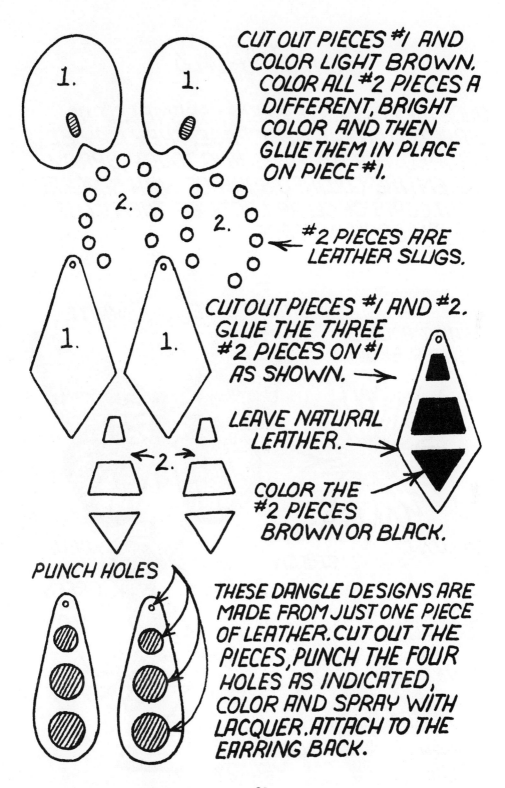

CUT OUT PIECES #1 AND COLOR LIGHT BROWN. COLOR ALL #2 PIECES A DIFFERENT, BRIGHT COLOR AND THEN GLUE THEM IN PLACE ON PIECE #1.

#2 PIECES ARE LEATHER SLUGS.

CUT OUT PIECES #1 AND #2. GLUE THE THREE #2 PIECES ON #1 AS SHOWN. →

LEAVE NATURAL LEATHER. →

COLOR THE #2 PIECES BROWN OR BLACK.

PUNCH HOLES

THESE DANGLE DESIGNS ARE MADE FROM JUST ONE PIECE OF LEATHER. CUT OUT THE PIECES, PUNCH THE FOUR HOLES AS INDICATED, COLOR AND SPRAY WITH LACQUER. ATTACH TO THE EARRING BACK.

91

Lapel Pins

ONCE THE PINS HAVE BEEN ASSEMBLED AS
DIRECTED ON THE NEXT PAGE, THEY MAY BE
COLORED. FOR THE FINISHING TOUCH, SPRAY
THE ENTIRE COLORED SURFACE WITH SEVERAL
LIGHT COATS OF CLEAR LACQUER. THEN GLUE
THE PIN BACK IN PLACE.

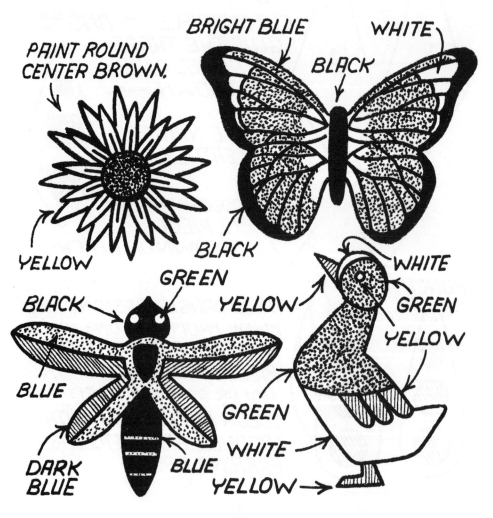

PAINT ROUND
CENTER BROWN.

YELLOW

BRIGHT BLUE

WHITE

BLACK

BLACK

GREEN

BLACK

YELLOW

WHITE

GREEN

YELLOW

BLUE

GREEN

DARK
BLUE

BLUE

WHITE

YELLOW

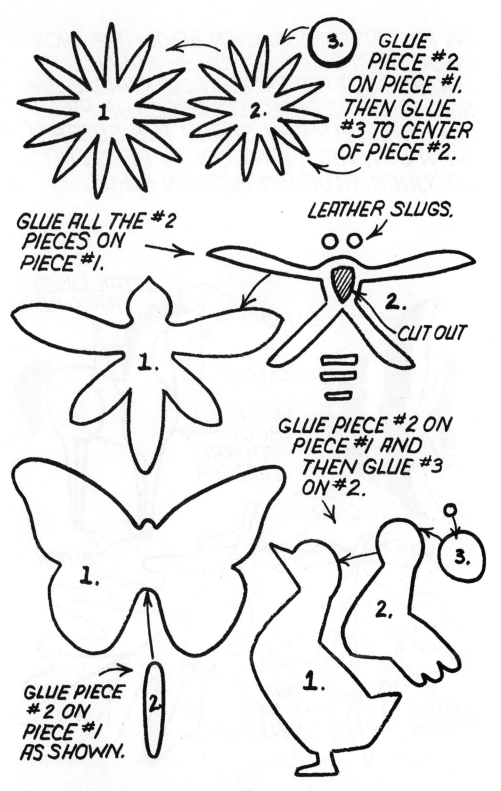

3. GLUE PIECE #2 ON PIECE #1. THEN GLUE #3 TO CENTER OF PIECE #2.

GLUE ALL THE #2 PIECES ON PIECE #1.

LEATHER SLUGS.

2.

CUT OUT

GLUE PIECE #2 ON PIECE #1 AND THEN GLUE #3 ON #2.

GLUE PIECE #2 ON PIECE #1 AS SHOWN.

THE PIN PATTERNS SHOWN BELOW ARE EACH
MADE FROM ONE PIECE OF 3-4 OUNCE
LEATHER. CUT THE PATTERN OUT CAREFULLY
AND COLOR AS DIRECTED. ONCE THE PAINT
IS COMPLETELY DRY, SPRAY THE SURFACE
WITH SEVERAL LIGHT COATS OF CLEAR
LACQUER. GLUE PIN BACK IN PLACE.

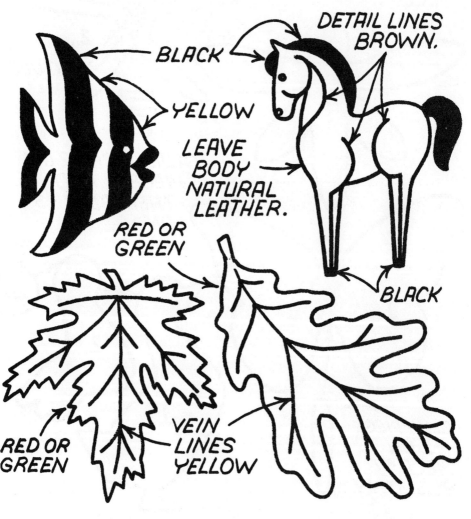

BLACK

DETAIL LINES
BROWN.

YELLOW

LEAVE
BODY
NATURAL
LEATHER.

RED OR
GREEN

BLACK

RED OR
GREEN

VEIN
LINES
YELLOW

Coasters

PATTERNS FOR THE COASTERS SHOWN BELOW
ARE ON THE FOLLOWING PAGES. CUT OUT THE
MAIN CIRCLE (3¼") AND PAINT IT A DARK
BROWN OR BLACK. ONCE THE PIECES #1 AND
2 HAVE BEEN GLUED IN POSITION ON THE
MAIN CIRCLE, SPRAY THE ENTIRE SURFACE,
LIGHTLY, WITH A CLEAR LACQUER.

CUT MAIN CIRCLE FROM 5-6 OUNCE LEATHER.
CUT PIECES #1 AND #2 FROM 3 OUNCE LEATHER.

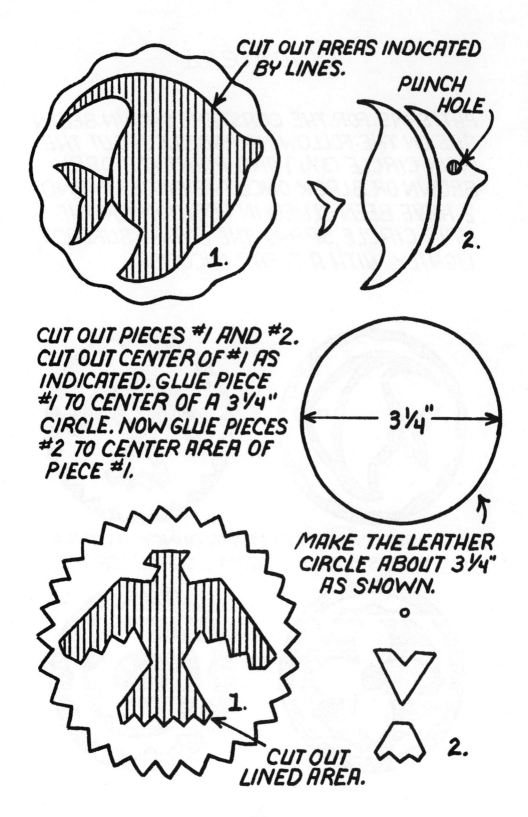

CUT OUT AREAS INDICATED BY LINES.

PUNCH HOLE

1.

2.

CUT OUT PIECES #1 AND #2. CUT OUT CENTER OF #1 AS INDICATED. GLUE PIECE #1 TO CENTER OF A 3¼" CIRCLE. NOW GLUE PIECES #2 TO CENTER AREA OF PIECE #1.

3¼"

MAKE THE LEATHER CIRCLE ABOUT 3¼" AS SHOWN.

1.

CUT OUT LINED AREA.

2.

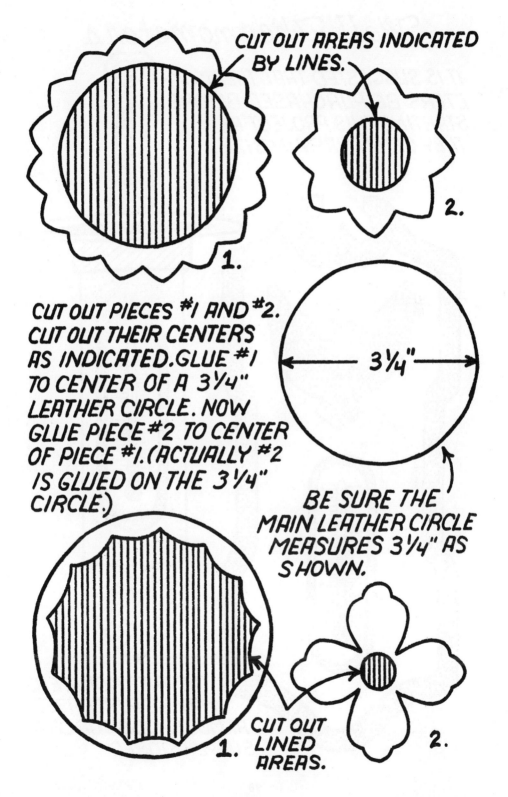

CUT OUT AREAS INDICATED BY LINES.

1.

2.

CUT OUT PIECES #1 AND #2. CUT OUT THEIR CENTERS AS INDICATED. GLUE #1 TO CENTER OF A 3¼" LEATHER CIRCLE. NOW GLUE PIECE #2 TO CENTER OF PIECE #1. (ACTUALLY #2 IS GLUED ON THE 3¼" CIRCLE.)

3¼"

BE SURE THE MAIN LEATHER CIRCLE MEASURES 3¼" AS SHOWN.

1.

CUT OUT LINED AREAS.

2.

Wall Thermometers

IT IS SUGGESTED THAT THERMOM-
ETERS BE PURCHASED BEFORE
STARTING THIS PROJECT AS
THEY OFTEN VARY IN SIZE.

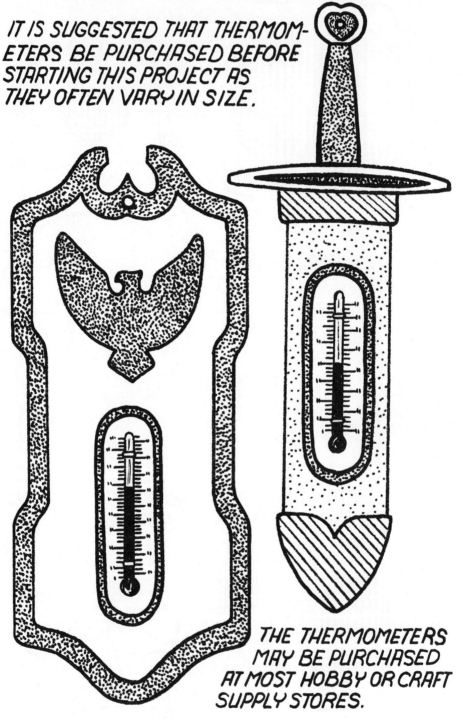

THE THERMOMETERS
MAY BE PURCHASED
AT MOST HOBBY OR CRAFT
SUPPLY STORES.

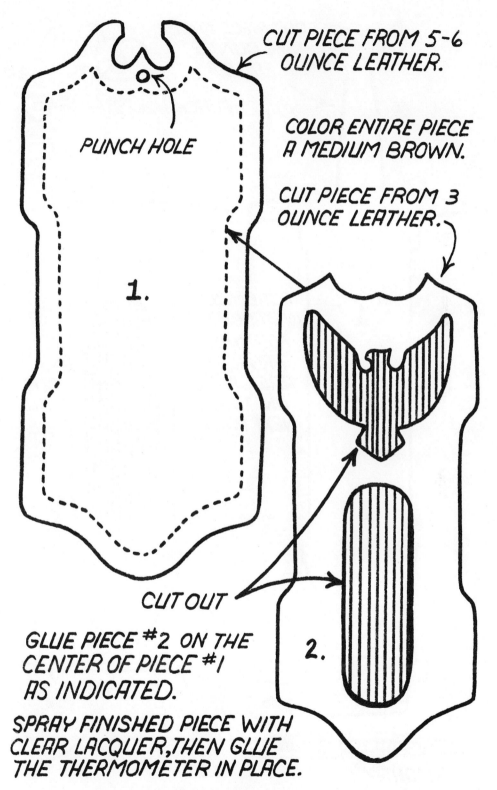

CUT PIECE FROM 5-6 OUNCE LEATHER.

COLOR ENTIRE PIECE A MEDIUM BROWN.

CUT PIECE FROM 3 OUNCE LEATHER.

PUNCH HOLE

1.

CUT OUT

2.

GLUE PIECE #2 ON THE CENTER OF PIECE #1 AS INDICATED.

SPRAY FINISHED PIECE WITH CLEAR LACQUER, THEN GLUE THE THERMOMETER IN PLACE.

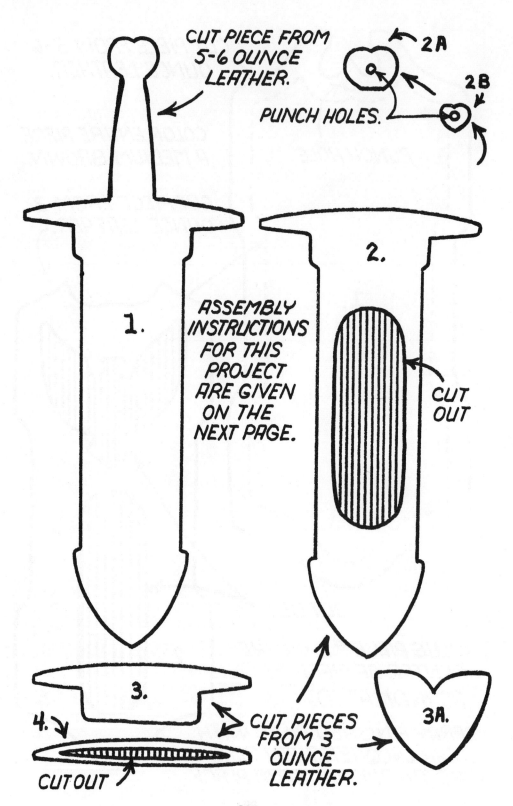

CUT PIECE FROM 5-6 OUNCE LEATHER.

2A

PUNCH HOLES.

2B

1.

ASSEMBLY INSTRUCTIONS FOR THIS PROJECT ARE GIVEN ON THE NEXT PAGE.

2.

CUT OUT

3.

4.

CUT OUT

CUT PIECES FROM 3 OUNCE LEATHER.

3A.

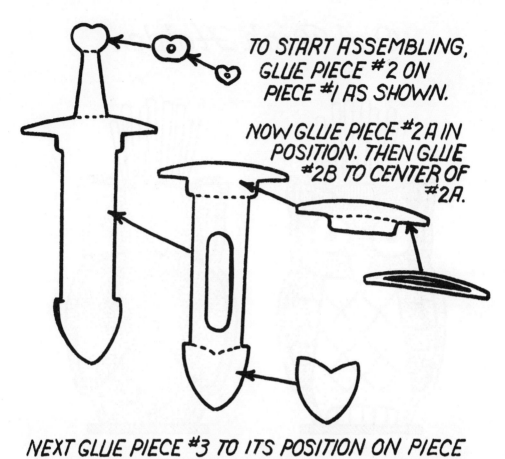

TO START ASSEMBLING, GLUE PIECE #2 ON PIECE #1 AS SHOWN.

NOW GLUE PIECE #2A IN POSITION. THEN GLUE #2B TO CENTER OF #2A.

NEXT GLUE PIECE #3 TO ITS POSITION ON PIECE #2. ALSO GLUE PIECE #3A TO THE LOWER PART OF #2 AS SHOWN ABOVE.

FINALLY GLUE PIECE #4 ON PIECE #3.

ONCE THE PROJECT HAS BEEN COMPLETELY ASSEMBLED, IT MAY BE COLORED. →

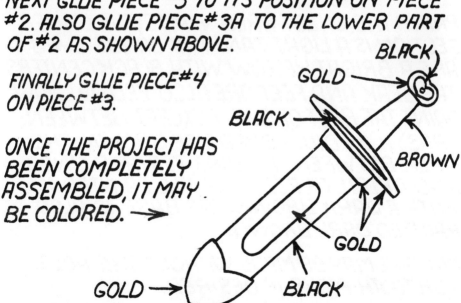

BLACK

GOLD →

BLACK →

BROWN

GOLD

GOLD →

BLACK

Owl Pick Holder

PAINT THE CHEST AREA WHITE; THE LOWER
SECTION IS A LIGHT TAN. THE LARGE EYES
ARE A BRIGHT YELLOW WITH BLACK CENTERS.
THE BEAK AND FEET ARE ALSO YELLOW. NOW
PAINT THE REST OF OWL (EXCEPT BETWEEN
EARS) A MEDIUM SHADE OF BROWN. THE
AREA BETWEEN THE EARS, FEATHER LINES
AND DETAIL OF FEET ARE ALL PAINTED IN
WITH A DARK BROWN. THE BASE IS ALSO
PAINTED DARK BROWN.

THE OWL MAY BE MADE WITHOUT THE HOLE
FOR TOOTH PICKS IF DESIRED.

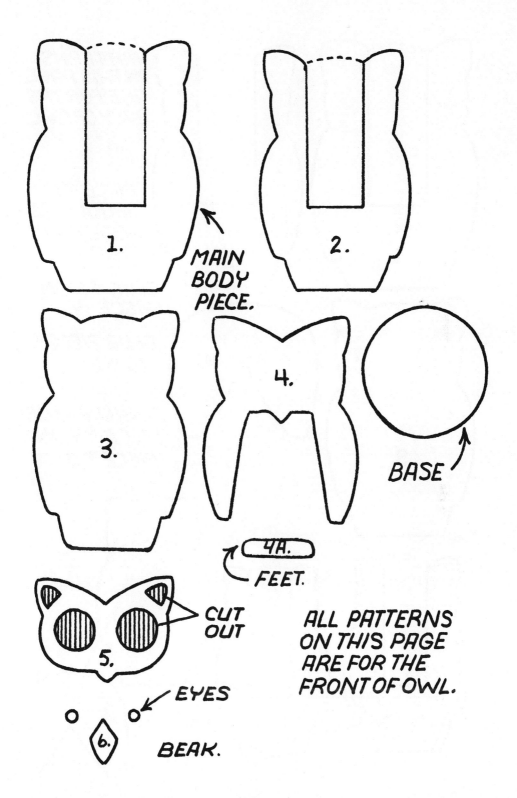

1.

2.

MAIN BODY PIECE.

3.

4.

BASE

4A. FEET.

5. CUT OUT

ALL PATTERNS ON THIS PAGE ARE FOR THE FRONT OF OWL.

EYES

6. BEAK.

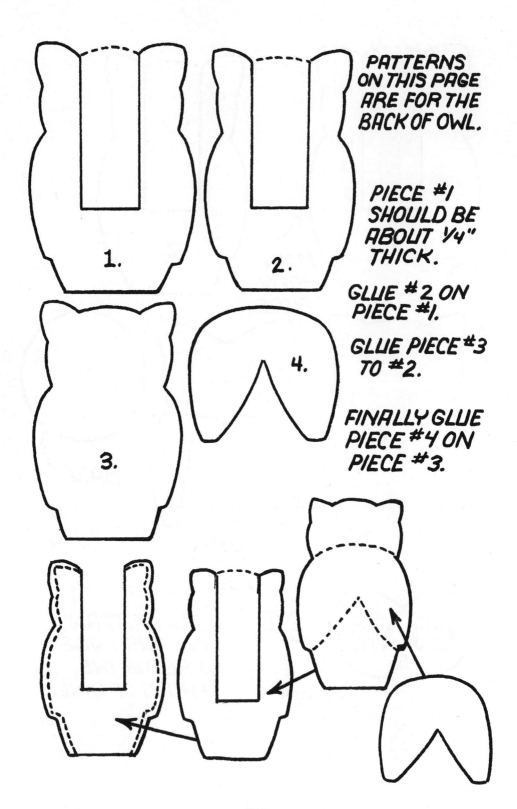

PATTERNS
ON THIS PAGE
ARE FOR THE
BACK OF OWL.

PIECE #1
SHOULD BE
ABOUT ¼"
THICK.

GLUE #2 ON
PIECE #1.

GLUE PIECE #3
TO #2.

FINALLY GLUE
PIECE #4 ON
PIECE #3.

1.

2.

3.

4.

BUILD UP PIECE #1 WITH SEVERAL PIECES OF LEATHER TO MAKE IT ABOUT 1/4" THICK.

NOW START TO ASSEMBLE THE OWL. GLUE PIECE #2 ON #1 AS SHOWN.

NEXT GLUE PIECE #3 ON #2.

GLUE PIECE #4 TO PIECE #3. ALSO GLUE #4A (FEET) IN PLACE ON #3 AS SHOWN.

NOW GLUE PIECE #5 (WITH THE ROUND EYE AND EAR AREAS CUT OUT) IN PLACE ON #4.

FINALLY GLUE THE BEAK ON PIECE #5. GLUE TWO SMALL LEATHER SLUGS TO CENTER OF CUTOUT CIRCLES IN #5.

GLUE FRONT AND BACK HALVES OF OWL TOGETHER.

NOW GLUE THE OWL TO CENTER OF BASE.

Rooster Pick Holder

WITH JUST THE ONE SET OF PATTERNS THIS ROOSTER CAN BE MADE TWO DIFFERENT WAYS.

WHEN THE ROOSTER HAS BEEN COMPLETELY ASSEMBLED AS DIRECTED, HE IS READY TO PAINT. THE MAIN BODY COLOR IS A REDDISH BROWN, WITH THE COMB, WING CENTER AND TAIL SECTION PAINTED A BRIGHT RED. THE BEAK IS YELLOW, THE EYES BLACK.

IF DESIRED, THE ROOSTER CAN BE MADE WITHOUT THE HOLE IN HIS BACK FOR THE TOOTH PICKS. NOTE THE DOTTED LINES ON PATTERN PIECES #1, 2 AND 3.

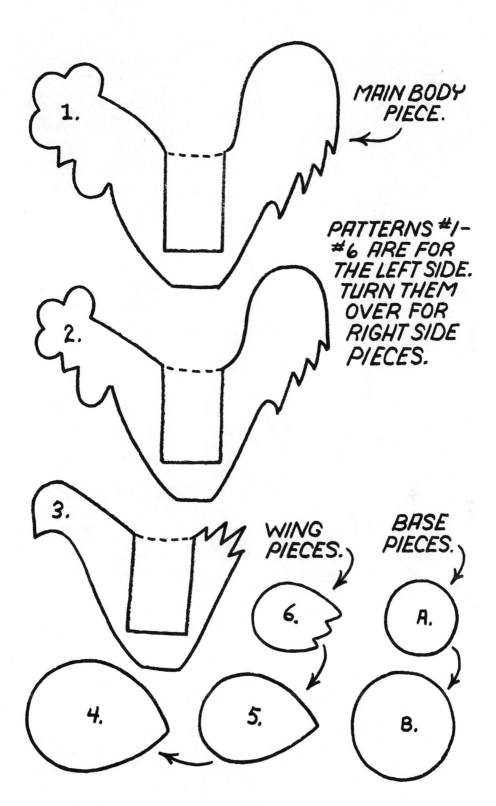

1.

MAIN BODY
PIECE.

PATTERNS #1–
#6 ARE FOR
THE LEFT SIDE.
TURN THEM
OVER FOR
RIGHT SIDE
PIECES.

2.

3.

WING
PIECES.

BASE
PIECES.

6.

A.

4.

5.

B.

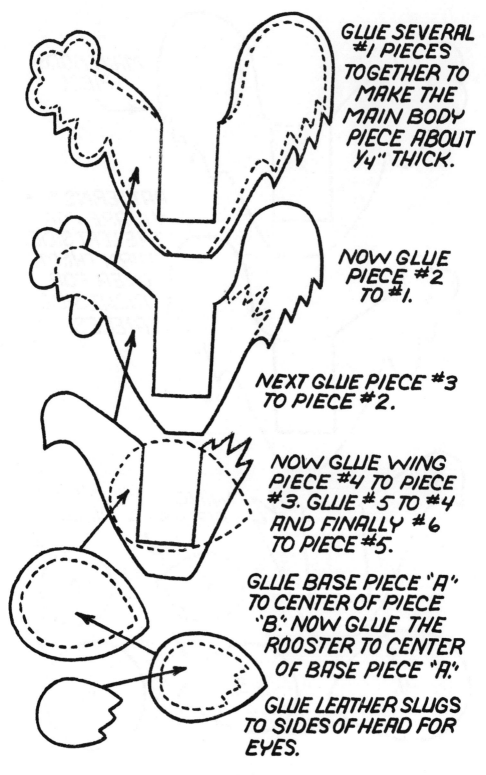

GLUE SEVERAL #1 PIECES TOGETHER TO MAKE THE MAIN BODY PIECE ABOUT 1/4" THICK.

NOW GLUE PIECE #2 TO #1.

NEXT GLUE PIECE #3 TO PIECE #2.

NOW GLUE WING PIECE #4 TO PIECE #3. GLUE #5 TO #4 AND FINALLY #6 TO PIECE #5.

GLUE BASE PIECE "A" TO CENTER OF PIECE "B." NOW GLUE THE ROOSTER TO CENTER OF BASE PIECE "A."

GLUE LEATHER SLUGS TO SIDES OF HEAD FOR EYES.

Little Cottontail

CUT OUT THE LEFT SIDE PATTERNS SHOWN ON THE NEXT PAGE AND ASSEMBLE AS DIRECTED. NOW TURN THE PATTERNS OVER AND CUT OUT ALL PIECES FOR THE RIGHT SIDE. ASSEMBLE RIGHT SIDE, THEN GLUE THE TWO HALVES TOGETHER. NOW GLUE THE TWO EARS TO THE SIDES OF HEAD AND THE COTTONTAIL IS READY TO PAINT, IF DESIRED.

TO PAINT THE ASSEMBLED COTTONTAIL, YOU WILL NEED THREE COLORS, WHITE, GREY AND BLACK. START BY PAINTING THE WHITE AREAS INDICATED ON THE ILLUSTRATION ABOVE. NOW PAINT THE REST OF THE COTTONTAIL WITH A MEDIUM GREY. ALLOW THE GREY TO OVERLAP THE WHITE SLIGHTLY.

GLUE ON TWO TINY LEATHER SLUGS FOR THE EYES. A PIECE OF COTTON IS GLUED TO THE LOWER BACK FOR A TAIL.

THIS LITTLE COTTONTAIL IS AN IDEAL EASTERTIME PROJECT.

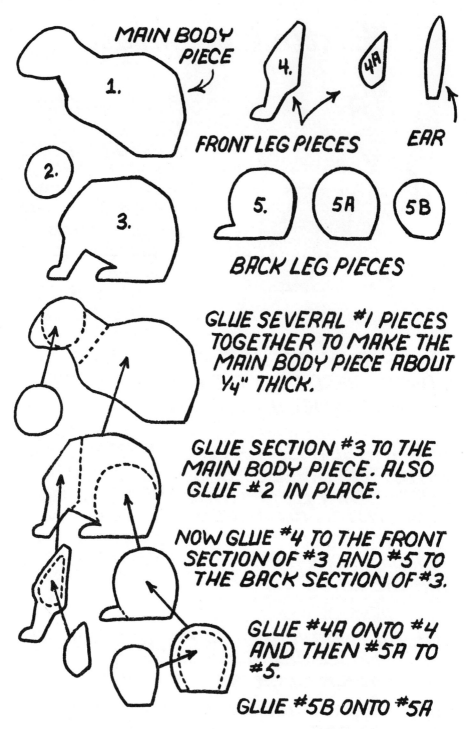

MAIN BODY PIECE

1.

FRONT LEG PIECES

EAR

4.

4A

2.

3.

5. 5A 5B

BACK LEG PIECES

GLUE SEVERAL #1 PIECES TOGETHER TO MAKE THE MAIN BODY PIECE ABOUT ¼" THICK.

GLUE SECTION #3 TO THE MAIN BODY PIECE. ALSO GLUE #2 IN PLACE.

NOW GLUE #4 TO THE FRONT SECTION OF #3 AND #5 TO THE BACK SECTION OF #3.

GLUE #4A ONTO #4 AND THEN #5A TO #5.

GLUE #5B ONTO #5A

GLUE EARS TO SIDES OF THE HEAD.

The Basset Hound

THE PATTERNS AND COMPLETE ASSEMBLY
INSTRUCTIONS FOR MAKING THIS LITTLE DOG
ARE GIVEN ON THE FOLLOWING TWO PAGES.

FOR PAINTING THE FINISHED HOUND YOU WILL
NEED THREE COLORS, MEDIUM BROWN, WHITE
AND BLACK. START BY PAINTING THE WHITE
AREAS, INDICATED ON THE ILLUSTRATION
ABOVE. NEXT PAINT ON THE LIGHT BROWN,
ALLOWING IT TO OVERLAP THE WHITE JUST
SLIGHTLY. NOW PAINT THE BACK OF HEAD,
TOP OF BACK AND TAIL BLACK. ALSO PAINT
THE NOSE AND EYES BLACK. LITTLE BLACK
NAILS CAN ALSO BE PAINTED ON THE FRONT
OF EACH FOOT AS SHOWN ON ILLUSTRATION.

MAKE THREE SMALL HOLES ON EACH SIDE OF
THE MUZZLE WITH AN AWL. COLOR THEM
BLACK.

BASSET PATTERNS

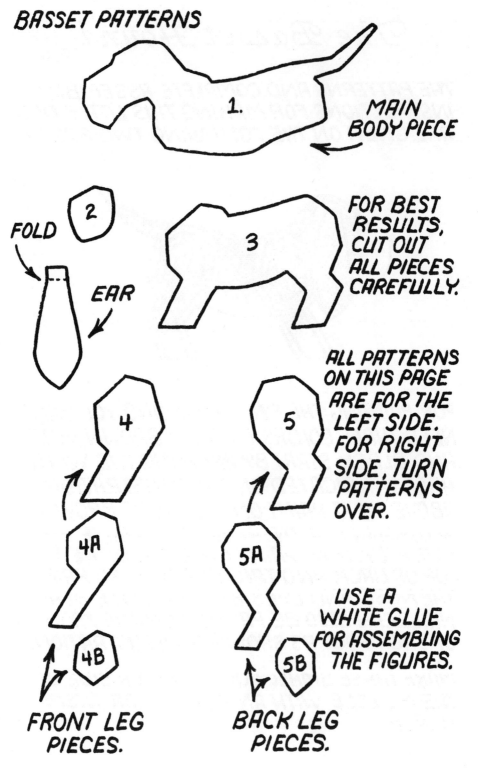

1. MAIN BODY PIECE

FOLD

2

EAR

3 FOR BEST RESULTS, CUT OUT ALL PIECES CAREFULLY.

4

5

ALL PATTERNS ON THIS PAGE ARE FOR THE LEFT SIDE. FOR RIGHT SIDE, TURN PATTERNS OVER.

4A

5A

USE A WHITE GLUE FOR ASSEMBLING THE FIGURES.

4B

5B

FRONT LEG PIECES.

BACK LEG PIECES.

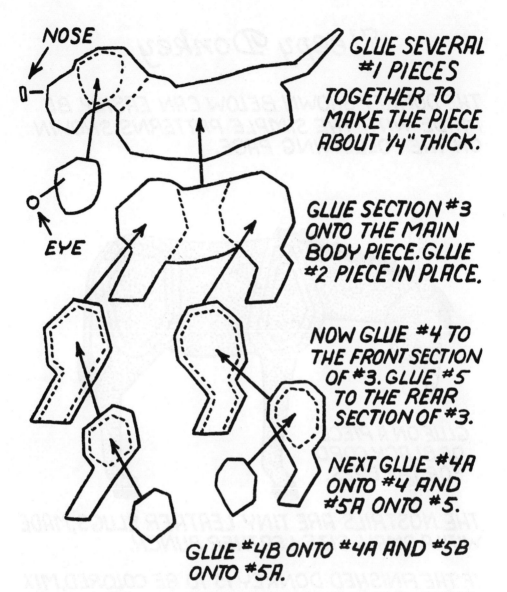

NOSE

EYE

GLUE SEVERAL #1 PIECES TOGETHER TO MAKE THE PIECE ABOUT ¼" THICK.

GLUE SECTION #3 ONTO THE MAIN BODY PIECE. GLUE #2 PIECE IN PLACE.

NOW GLUE #4 TO THE FRONT SECTION OF #3. GLUE #5 TO THE REAR SECTION OF #3.

NEXT GLUE #4A ONTO #4 AND #5A ONTO #5.

GLUE #4B ONTO #4A AND #5B ONTO #5A.

REPEAT THESE SAME STEPS TO ASSEMBLE THE RIGHT SIDE. THEN GLUE THE TWO IDENTICAL HALVES TOGETHER.

FOLD EARS WHERE INDICATED AND GLUE TO HEAD. GLUE ON TINY LEATHER SLUGS FOR THE EYES AND NOSE.

Sleepy Donkey

THE DONKEY SHOWN BELOW CAN EASILY BE
MADE WITH THE SIMPLE PATTERNS SHOWN
ON THE FOLLOWING PAGE.

GLUE ON A PIECE
OF BLACK CORD
FOR THE EYES.

THE NOSTRILS ARE TINY LEATHER SLUGS, MADE
WITH A SMALL SIZE LEATHER PUNCH.

IF THE FINISHED DONKEY IS TO BE COLORED, MIX
BLACK AND WHITE TOGETHER UNTIL A MEDIUM
GREY IS ACHIEVED. PAINT ENTIRE BODY WITH
THE GREY, EXCEPT AROUND THE EYES AND THE
MUZZLE. COLOR THESE AREAS A VERY LIGHT
GREY. COLOR THE MANE, FORELOCK, HOOFS AND
END OF TAIL A DARK GREY OR BLACK.

THE DONKEY DOES NOT REQUIRE A BASE.

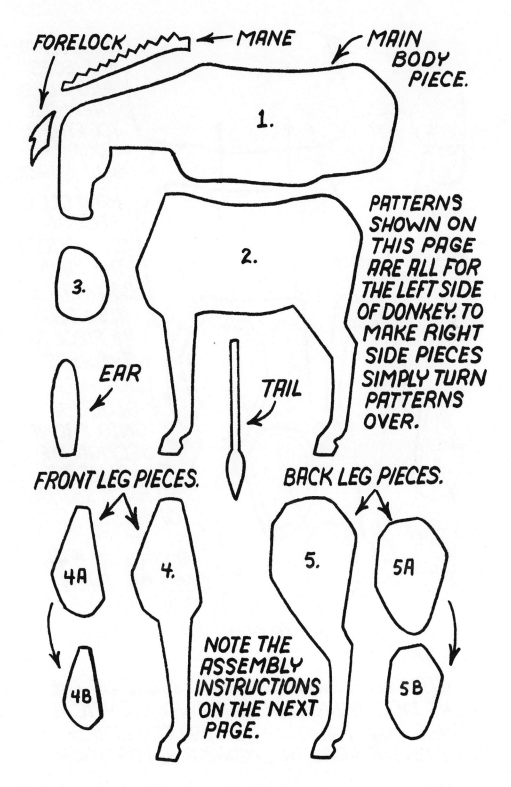

FORELOCK — MANE — MAIN BODY PIECE.

1.

PATTERNS SHOWN ON THIS PAGE ARE ALL FOR THE LEFT SIDE OF DONKEY. TO MAKE RIGHT SIDE PIECES SIMPLY TURN PATTERNS OVER.

2.

3.

EAR

TAIL

FRONT LEG PIECES.

BACK LEG PIECES.

4A

4.

5.

5A

4B

NOTE THE ASSEMBLY INSTRUCTIONS ON THE NEXT PAGE.

5B

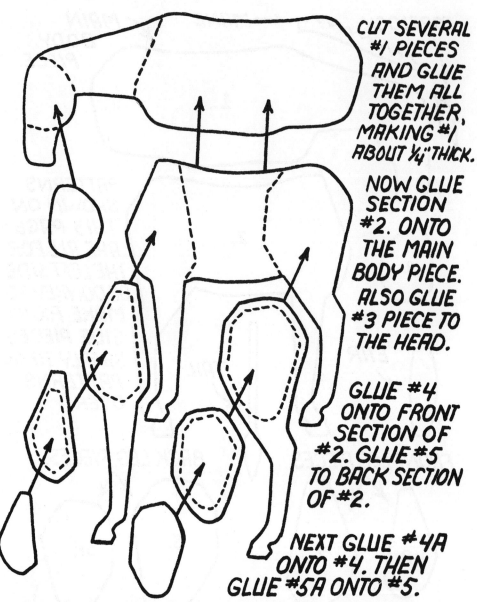

CUT SEVERAL #1 PIECES AND GLUE THEM ALL TOGETHER, MAKING #1 ABOUT ¼" THICK.

NOW GLUE SECTION #2. ONTO THE MAIN BODY PIECE. ALSO GLUE #3 PIECE TO THE HEAD.

GLUE #4 ONTO FRONT SECTION OF #2. GLUE #5 TO BACK SECTION OF #2.

NEXT GLUE #4A ONTO #4. THEN GLUE #5A ONTO #5.

LAST OF ALL, GLUE #4B ONTO #4A AND THEN #5B ONTO #5A.

REPEAT THESE SAME STEPS TO MAKE UP THE RIGHT SIDE. THEN GLUE THE TWO IDENTICAL HALVES (RIGHT AND LEFT SIDES) TOGETHER. GLUE ON THE EARS, TAIL, MANE AND FORELOCK.

Jumbo

COMPLETE PATTERNS FOR MAKING JUMBO ARE
FOUND ON THE NEXT PAGES.

ONCE JUMBO HAS BEEN ASSEMBLED, MAKE A
SMALL HOLE IN EACH SIDE OF LOWER HEAD
WITH AN AWL. THEN INSERT SMALL PIECES OF
ROUND TOOTH PICK FOR THE TUSK. NOW
MAKE ANOTHER HOLE IN THE CENTER OF THE
LOWER BACK AND INSERT A SHORT PIECE OF
ROUND TOOTH PICK FOR THE TAIL.

GLUE A TINY LEATHER SLUG TO EACH SIDE OF
THE HEAD FOR EYES.

PAINT JUMBO WITH A MEDIUM GREY. PAINT
THE TUSK WHITE, EYES BLACK.

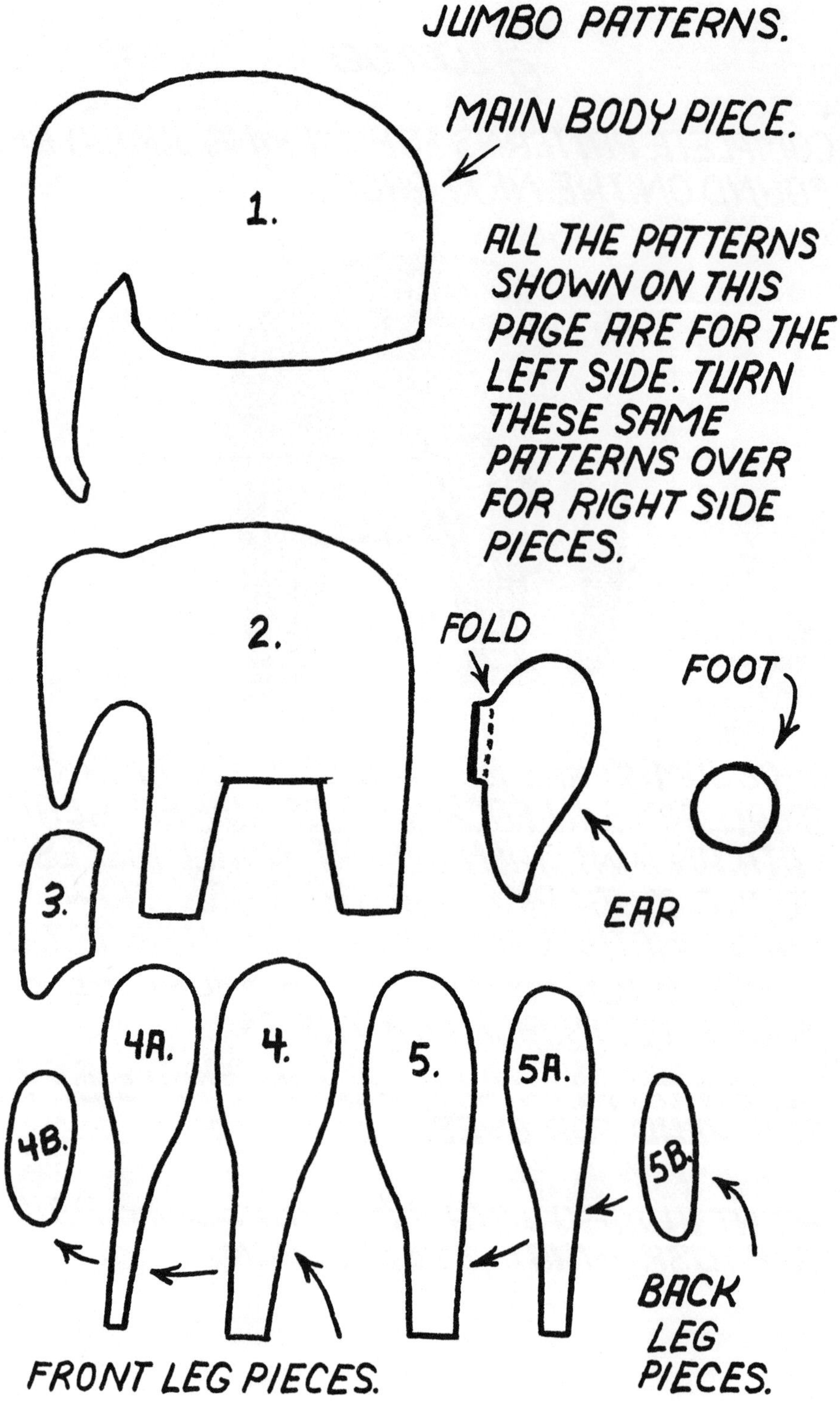

JUMBO PATTERNS.

MAIN BODY PIECE.

1.

ALL THE PATTERNS
SHOWN ON THIS
PAGE ARE FOR THE
LEFT SIDE. TURN
THESE SAME
PATTERNS OVER
FOR RIGHT SIDE
PIECES.

2.

FOLD

FOOT

3.

EAR

4B.

4A.

4.

5.

5A.

5B.

FRONT LEG PIECES.

BACK
LEG
PIECES.

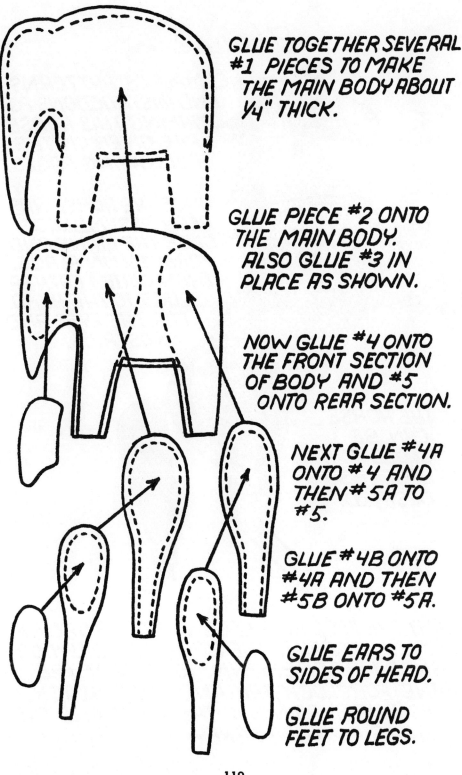

GLUE TOGETHER SEVERAL #1 PIECES TO MAKE THE MAIN BODY ABOUT ¼" THICK.

GLUE PIECE #2 ONTO THE MAIN BODY. ALSO GLUE #3 IN PLACE AS SHOWN.

NOW GLUE #4 ONTO THE FRONT SECTION OF BODY AND #5 ONTO REAR SECTION.

NEXT GLUE #4A ONTO #4 AND THEN #5A TO #5.

GLUE #4B ONTO #4A AND THEN #5B ONTO #5A.

GLUE EARS TO SIDES OF HEAD.

GLUE ROUND FEET TO LEGS.

Horse

COMPLETE PATTERNS AND INSTRUCTIONS FOR MAKING THIS HORSE ARE GIVEN ON THE FOLLOWING PAGES.

ONCE THE HORSE HAS BEEN ASSEMBLED, GLUE THE MANE AND FORELOCK IN PLACE. THEN GLUE LEATHER SLUGS TO THE HEAD FOR THE EYES AND NOSTRILS.

THE HORSE CAN BE GLUED TO A BASE, IF SO DESIRED.

PAINT THE FACE AND LEGS WHITE AS SHOWN ABOVE. NEXT PAINT THE BODY A MEDIUM OR LIGHT SHADE OF BROWN. NOW PAINT THE MANE, FORELOCK, TAIL AND EYES BLACK. FINISH UP BY PAINTING THE HOOFS AND THE NOSTRILS A MEDIUM GREY.

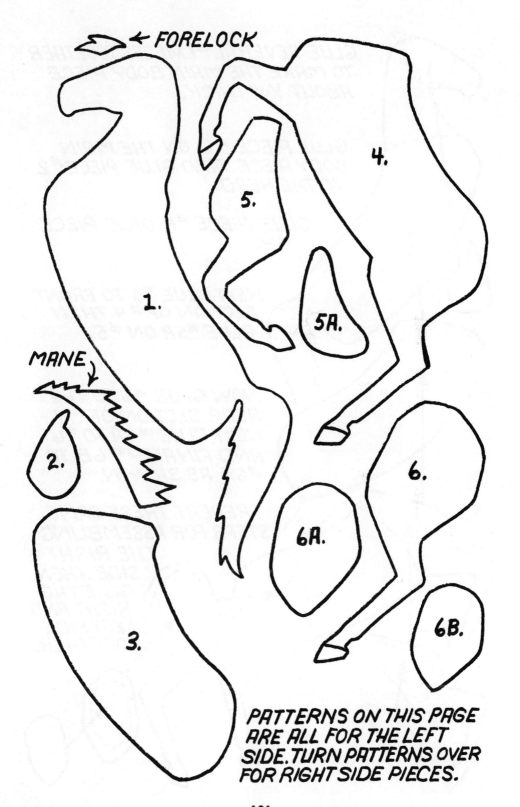

FORELOCK

MANE

1.

2.

3.

4.

5.

5A.

6.

6A.

6B.

PATTERNS ON THIS PAGE
ARE ALL FOR THE LEFT
SIDE. TURN PATTERNS OVER
FOR RIGHT SIDE PIECES.

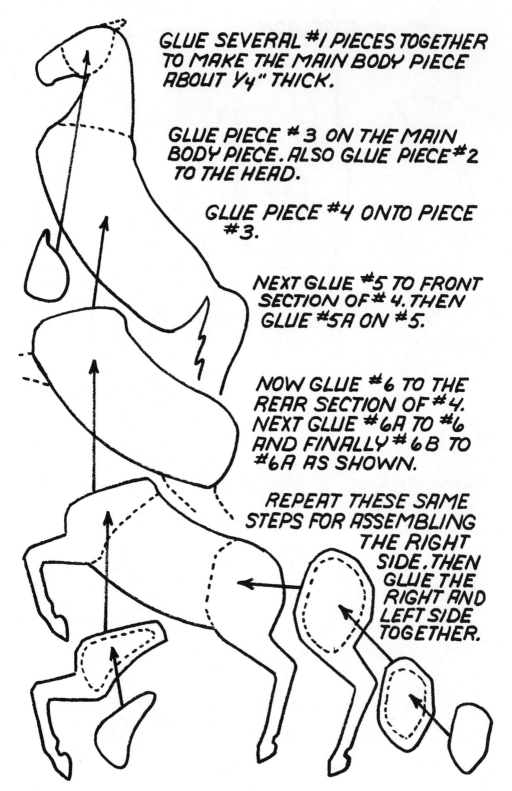

GLUE SEVERAL #1 PIECES TOGETHER TO MAKE THE MAIN BODY PIECE ABOUT 1/4" THICK.

GLUE PIECE #3 ON THE MAIN BODY PIECE. ALSO GLUE PIECE #2 TO THE HEAD.

GLUE PIECE #4 ONTO PIECE #3.

NEXT GLUE #5 TO FRONT SECTION OF #4. THEN GLUE #5A ON #5.

NOW GLUE #6 TO THE REAR SECTION OF #4. NEXT GLUE #6A TO #6 AND FINALLY #6B TO #6A AS SHOWN.

REPEAT THESE SAME STEPS FOR ASSEMBLING THE RIGHT SIDE. THEN GLUE THE RIGHT AND LEFT SIDE TOGETHER.

Bear

BEFORE STARTING TO MAKE THE BEAR, NOTICE THAT THE RIGHT AND LEFT SIDE PATTERNS ARE NOT THE SAME.

BECAUSE THE BEAR HAS BEEN DESIGNED IN A WALKING POSITION, THE RIGHT AND LEFT SIDES ARE DIFFERENT. ASSEMBLE BOTH SIDES IN THE SAME STEPS DESCRIBED AND THEN GLUE THE TWO COMPLETELY ASSEMBLED HALVES TOGETHER. THE BEAR SHOULD NOW LOOK LIKE THE ILLUSTRATION ABOVE.

THE ASSEMBLED BEAR CAN BE PAINTED ALL BLACK OR A MEDIUM BROWN.

A BEAR CUB CAN EASILY BE MADE TO GO WITH THE BIG BEAR ABOVE BY REDUCING THE PATTERN'S SIZE WITH A PANTOGRAPH

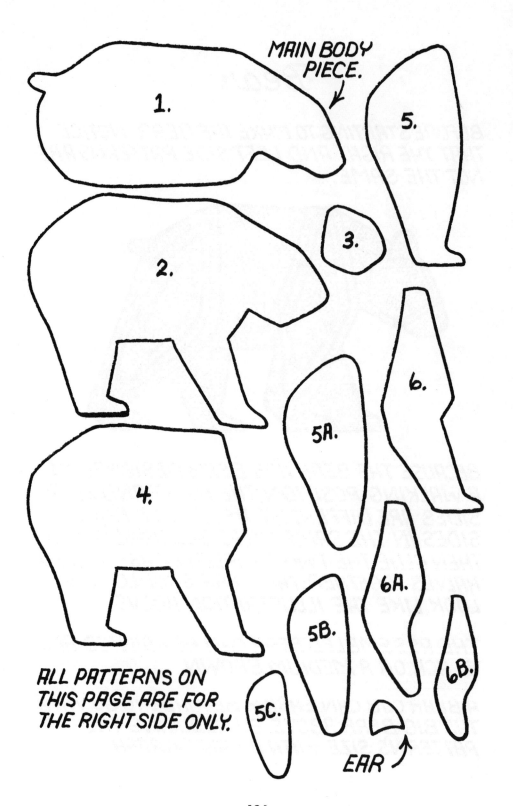

MAIN BODY
PIECE.

1.

5.

2.

3.

5A.

6.

4.

6A.

5B.

ALL PATTERNS ON
THIS PAGE ARE FOR
THE RIGHT SIDE ONLY.

5C.

6B.

EAR

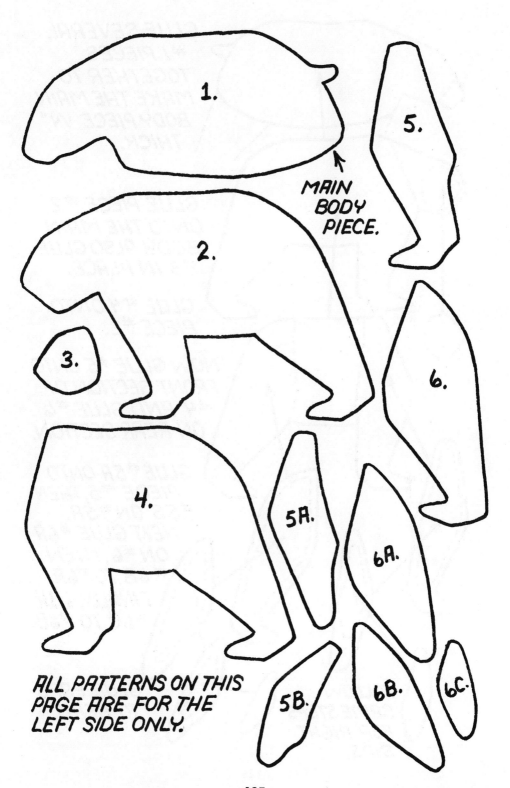

1.

MAIN
BODY
PIECE.

5.

2.

3.

6.

4.

5A.

6A.

ALL PATTERNS ON THIS
PAGE ARE FOR THE
LEFT SIDE ONLY.

5B.

6B.

6C.

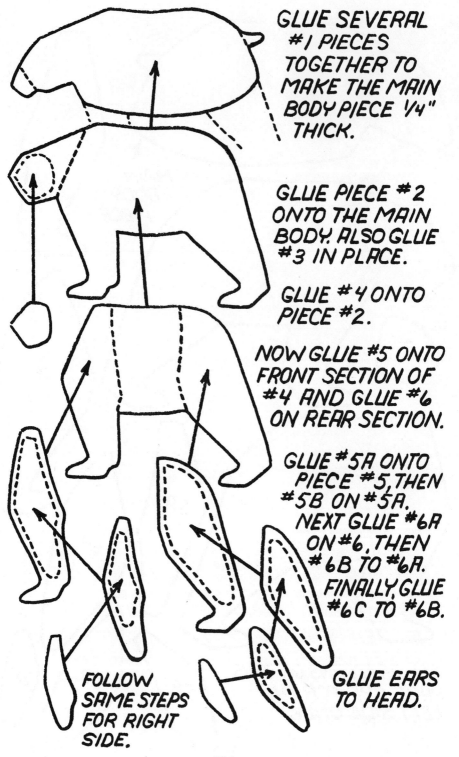

GLUE SEVERAL #1 PIECES TOGETHER TO MAKE THE MAIN BODY PIECE 1/4" THICK.

GLUE PIECE #2 ONTO THE MAIN BODY. ALSO GLUE #3 IN PLACE.

GLUE #4 ONTO PIECE #2.

NOW GLUE #5 ONTO FRONT SECTION OF #4 AND GLUE #6 ON REAR SECTION.

GLUE #5A ONTO PIECE #5, THEN #5B ON #5A. NEXT GLUE #6A ON #6, THEN #6B TO #6A. FINALLY, GLUE #6C TO #6B.

FOLLOW SAME STEPS FOR RIGHT SIDE.

GLUE EARS TO HEAD.

Roadrunner

NOTE THAT THE ROADRUNNER REQUIRES DIFFERENT RIGHT AND LEFT PATTERNS DUE TO HIS LEG POSITIONS.

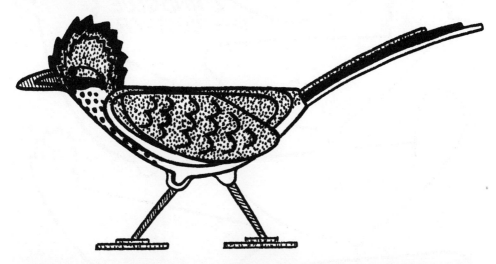

WHEN THE ROADRUNNER HAS BEEN ASSEMBLED AS DIRECTED, GLUE LEATHER SLUGS TO HEAD FOR EYES AND HE IS READY TO PAINT.

START BY PAINTING THE WHITE AREAS SHOWN ON THE ILLUSTRATION ABOVE. NOW PAINT THE BODY WITH A GREY-BROWN. WITH THIS SAME COLOR, PAINT ROUND SPOTS ON WHITE CHEST AREA. THE BLACK AREAS INDICATED ON THE ILLUSTRATION ARE PAINTED A BROWN-BLACK. PAINT AREA BEHIND EYE RED. THE BEAK, LEGS AND FEET ARE PAINTED A MEDIUM GREY.

CHILDREN'S COLORED BIRD BOOKS ARE AN EXCELLENT REFERENCE SOURCE FOR TRUE COLORS.

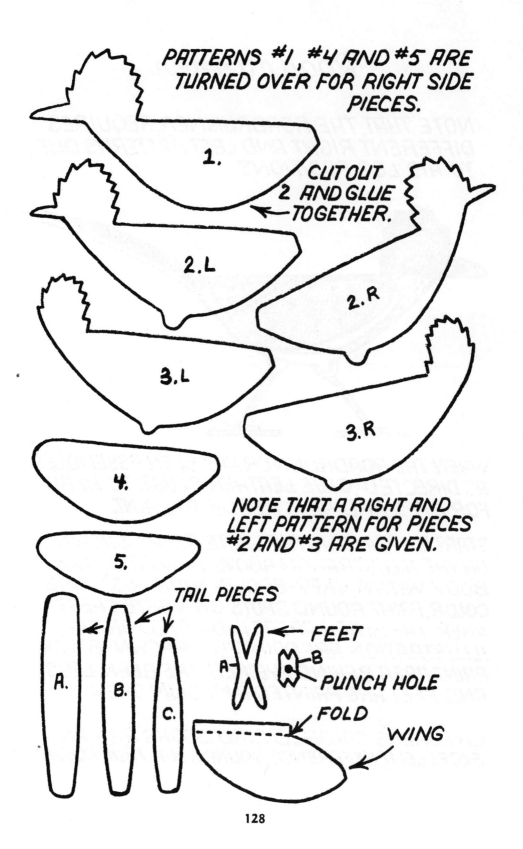

PATTERNS #1, #4 AND #5 ARE TURNED OVER FOR RIGHT SIDE PIECES.

1.

CUT OUT 2 AND GLUE TOGETHER.

2.L

2.R

3.L

3.R

4.

NOTE THAT A RIGHT AND LEFT PATTERN FOR PIECES #2 AND #3 ARE GIVEN.

5.

TAIL PIECES

A.

B.

C.

FEET

A

B

PUNCH HOLE

FOLD

WING

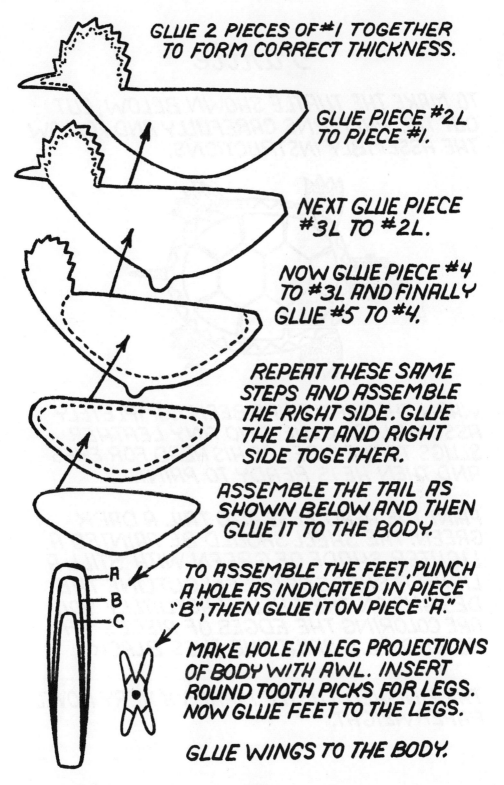

GLUE 2 PIECES OF #1 TOGETHER TO FORM CORRECT THICKNESS.

GLUE PIECE #2L TO PIECE #1.

NEXT GLUE PIECE #3L TO #2L.

NOW GLUE PIECE #4 TO #3L AND FINALLY GLUE #5 TO #4.

REPEAT THESE SAME STEPS AND ASSEMBLE THE RIGHT SIDE. GLUE THE LEFT AND RIGHT SIDE TOGETHER.

ASSEMBLE THE TAIL AS SHOWN BELOW AND THEN GLUE IT TO THE BODY.

TO ASSEMBLE THE FEET, PUNCH A HOLE AS INDICATED IN PIECE "B", THEN GLUE IT ON PIECE "A."

MAKE HOLE IN LEG PROJECTIONS OF BODY WITH AWL. INSERT ROUND TOOTH PICKS FOR LEGS. NOW GLUE FEET TO THE LEGS.

GLUE WINGS TO THE BODY.

129

Turtle

TO MAKE THE TURTLE SHOWN BELOW, CUT OUT THE PATTERNS CAREFULLY AND FOLLOW THE ASSEMBLY INSTRUCTIONS.

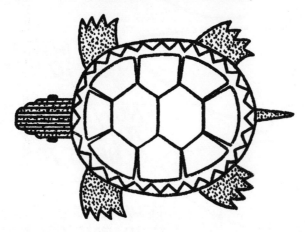

WHEN THE TURTLE HAS BEEN COMPLETELY ASSEMBLED, GLUE TWO TINY LEATHER SLUGS TO THE SIDES OF HIS HEAD FOR EYES AND THEN HE IS READY TO PAINT.

PAINT THE HEAD, LEGS AND TAIL A DARK GREEN. THE SHELL SHOULD BE PAINTED A LIGHTER SHADE OF GREEN. WITH STILL A LIGHTER SHADE OF GREEN, OUTLINE THE DESIGNS ON THE SHELL. (ACTUALLY YOU ARE COLORING THE EDGES OF PIECES #4 #5 AND #6.) PAINT THE EYES BLACK.

THE FINISHED TURTLE MAKES A VERY NOVEL PAPERWEIGHT.

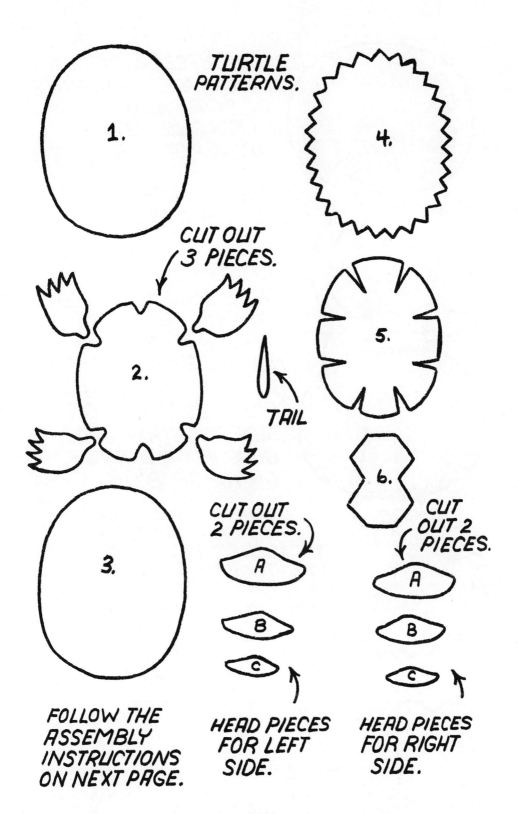

TURTLE
PATTERNS.

1.

4.

CUT OUT
3 PIECES.

2.

TAIL

5.

6.

CUT OUT
2 PIECES.

A

B

C

CUT
OUT 2
PIECES.

A

B

C

3.

FOLLOW THE
ASSEMBLY
INSTRUCTIONS
ON NEXT PAGE.

HEAD PIECES
FOR LEFT
SIDE.

HEAD PIECES
FOR RIGHT
SIDE.

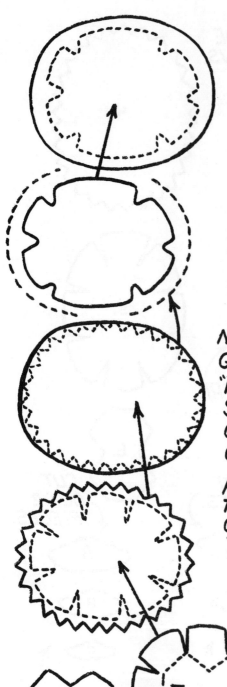

GLUE PIECE #2 (MADE 3
LAYERS THICK) TO CENTER
OF #1 AS SHOWN.
 NOW GLUE PIECE #3
ON TOP OF #2.

NEXT GLUE PIECE #4
ON TOP OF #3.

GLUE #5 ON TOP OF #4
THEN GLUE #6 ON TOP
OF #5.

NOW ASSEMBLE THE HEAD.
GLUE THE TWO IDENTICAL
"A" PIECES OF THE LEFT
SIDE TOGETHER. NEXT
GLUE "B" ON "A" AND "C"
ON TOP OF "B."

REPEAT SAME STEPS FOR
THE RIGHT SIDE, THEN
GLUE THE TWO HALVES
TOGETHER.

NOW GLUE HEAD, TAIL
AND LEGS INTO THE
 PROPER LOCATIONS
 MADE IN PIECE
 #2.

Pork Chops

TO MAKE THIS FAT LITTLE PORK CHOPS, SIMPLY FOLLOW THE STEP-BY-STEP DIRECTIONS GIVEN ON THE FOLLOWING PAGES.

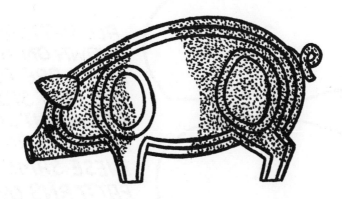

ONCE ALL THE LEFT SIDE BODY PIECES HAVE BEEN GLUED TOGETHER AS DESCRIBED, FOLLOW THE SAME STEPS AND GLUE TOGETHER ALL THE RIGHT SIDE PIECES. GLUE THE TWO IDENTICAL BODY HALVES TOGETHER AND PORK CHOPS WILL BE COMPLETE EXCEPT FOR HIS EARS AND TAIL. USE A PIECE OF LACE OR HEAVY CORD FOR THE TAIL. GLUE THE EARS IN POSITION.

COLOR PORK CHOPS BLACK AND WHITE AS SHOWN, OR IF DESIRED IT MAY BE COLORED ALL BLACK, BROWN, PINK OR EVEN WHITE. AFTER THE WATER COLOR IS DRY, SPRAY PIG WITH CLEAR LACQUER.

BY REDUCING THE PATTERNS TO HALF SIZE, BABY PIGS ARE EASILY MADE TO GO WITH PORK CHOPS.

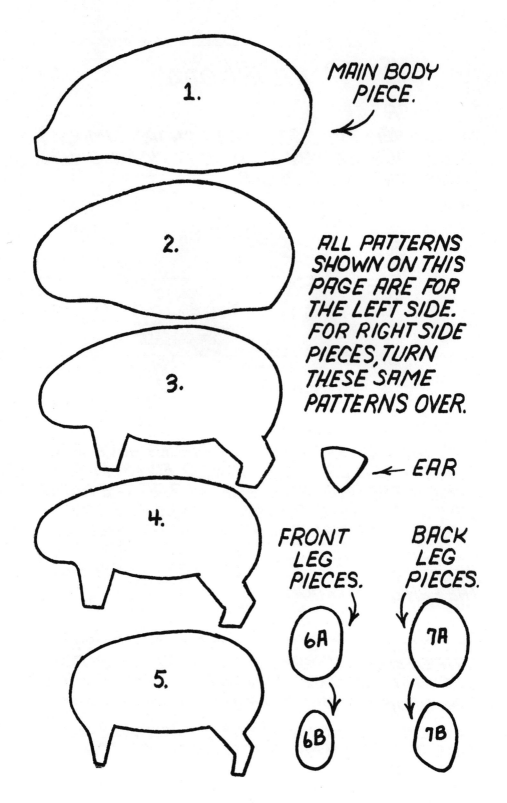

1.

MAIN BODY PIECE.

2.

ALL PATTERNS SHOWN ON THIS PAGE ARE FOR THE LEFT SIDE. FOR RIGHT SIDE PIECES, TURN THESE SAME PATTERNS OVER.

3.

← EAR

4.

FRONT LEG PIECES.

BACK LEG PIECES.

6A

7A

5.

6B

7B

GLUE SEVERAL
#1 PIECES
TOGETHER TO
MAKE THE
MAIN BODY
ABOUT 1/4"
THICK.

GLUE PIECE #2
ONTO THE MAIN
BODY PIECE.

NEXT GLUE #3
ONTO #2 AS
SHOWN.

GLUE PIECE #4
ONTO #3.

GLUE #5
ONTO #4.

GLUE #6A ONTO
FRONT SECTION
OF #5. GLUE
#7A TO REAR
SECTION.

GLUE #6B TO #6A
AND #7B TO #7A.

NOSE

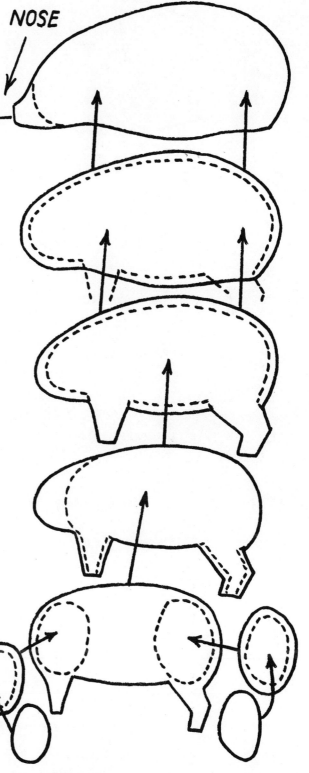

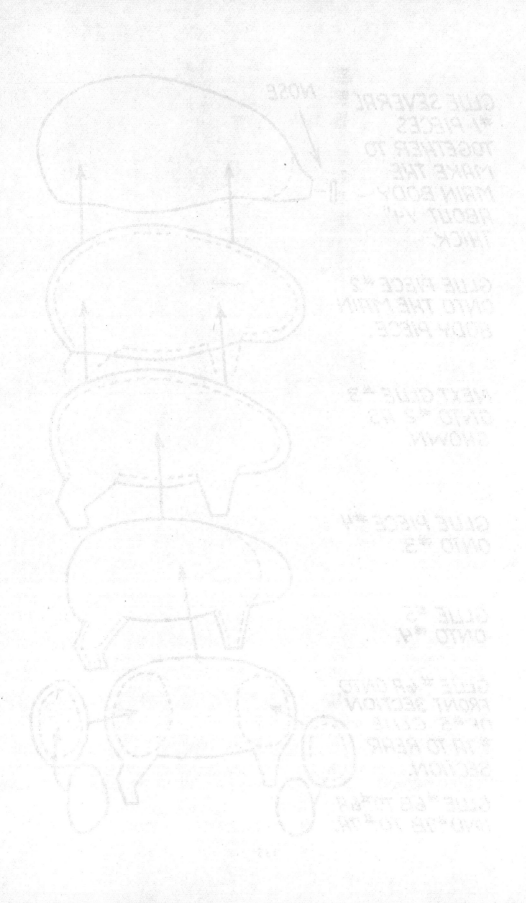